21

Anita Gates

STEPS TO A BETTER JOB

MONARCH PRESS NEW YORK

Published by MONARCH PRESS
A Division of Simon & Schuster, Inc.
Simon & Schuster Building
1230 Avenue of the Americas
New York, New York 10020

MONARCH PRESS and colophon are registered trademarks of
Simon & Schuster, Inc.
Designed by Irving Perkins Associates
Manufactured in the United States of America
10 9 8 7 6 5 4 3 2 1

Library of Congress Catalog Card Number: 83-61798
ISBN: 0-671-49364-7

Special thanks to the career experts whose professional advice appears on these pages, particularly to Linda Kline of Kline-McKay, career counselor Dr. James F. Malone, Gary Marshall of Smyth Dawson Associates and Tom Tepe of Bankers Trust. Their contributions go far beyond any direct quotes attributed to them.

Thanks also to the many businesspeople who shared their valuable experiences in hiring and being hired. They include Carolyn Culbreth, Richard Flagg, Jerrianne Hammock, Bruce Haxthausen and Anne Sweeney.

Personal thanks to Dominick Abel, my agent; Valerie Levy, my editor; Max Peace, who introduced me to many of the experts quoted on these pages; and to a small circle of friends—particularly Ellen Anderson, Karen Styles, and David Swindell—who seem to know when encouragement is needed.

CONTENTS

INTRODUCTION

Some people just seem to walk into great job offers. One day the phone rings, and it's a headhunter describing the perfect opportunity at the perfect salary. Other people may stagnate in the wrong job for years before they somehow manage to make a change. Some of them claim they'd have to be unemployed to find the time for all the interviews and contact-making required. After all, they contend, "job hunting is a full-time career."

But it's not. At least it doesn't have to be, if you know how to devote a little time each day, or a few hours twice a week, to setting things in motion. Launching a job search is a lot like starting an exercise program. Fifteen sit-ups a day or five minutes of aerobics every morning may not seem like much, but as the weeks and months go by the results can be seen.

As with a list of exercises, you may not want or need to make every step in this book a part of your program. For example, some people are naturally great interview subjects. If you're one of them, you can skip the sections on interview techniques, but only because you're strong in that area already.

And just as stomach exercises also affect your lower back, all the steps of job hunting work together. You may have written a résumé that could win national awards but, if you don't make the right contacts, you needn't have bothered. Without an "in," your résumé may be read only by clerks or entry-level personnel interviewers who won't recognize brilliance when they see it. Or you may have networked your way to an introduction to the president of MCI or IBM but, if your interviewing skills fall short, you'll waste the value of that introduction.

THE JOY OF NETWORKS

A smart job hunter will use every method available—agencies, search firms, classified ads—but for the vast majority, jobs are won by networking. Unfortunately, the term is overused and often misunderstood. When networking first emerged as a buzzword, particularly among working women, people set up formal networks that would meet like garden clubs every Monday or Tuesday night. People may have made business contacts, but they weren't networking in its truest—or most effective—sense.

The way it has worked for centuries is much simpler. People do things for others because they like them, know them well or owe them a favor. Every one of the career experts quoted in this book was recommended to me by a friend or business associate. And of the dozens of gainfully employed men and women interviewed, only one claimed to have gotten her current job without any personal contact to ease the way.

Even when people were placed in jobs by more traditional methods, like personnel agencies, the personal element had played a role. One woman's husband had known the agency executive who was handling the job. One man had worked with the hiring manager on numerous projects while employed by another corporation.

As one career counselor puts it, "It's not who you know; it's who knows you." Parents who once reminded marriageable daughters that it's as easy to fall in love with a rich man as a poor one may want to extend that parental advice: It's just as easy to make friends with successful or career-influential people you genuinely like and respect as it is to make friends with those who have nothing to do with your work.

THE TRENDS CHANGE QUICKLY

In job hunting, as in clothing, music and advertising design, trends change much faster than some realize.

If you haven't looked for a new job in several years, or if

you've made the last few moves up the career ladder without
having to mount a full-fledged campaign, these suggestions
may sound new:

- Send out a broadcast letter to employers without a résumé.
- Write a functional résumé without dates, but with lots
  of dollar-figure accomplishments.
- Impress interviewers by quoting the sales figures you
  read in their annual report.

Even if you never heard of these ideas, the people who are
hiring you have—so much so that they've grown suspicious
of them. Most recruiters see hundreds of thousands of résumés
per month. Ideas that seemed bright and inventive a few years
ago may now appear trite and obvious.

In 1962 public relations entrepreneur Betty Vaughn sent
out a résumé in the form of a coloring book, and as a result
signed on accounts that launched her own business. In 1983
an unemployed PR rep handed out leaflets containing his job
qualifications to commuters at Grand Central Station. The effort didn't result in a single interview, but a syndicated newspaper column featured him as an example of a job hunter taking "desperate measures." While unconventional job hunting
methods may still work on occasion, for the most part there's
been a return to more traditional approaches: formal chronological résumés, conservative business suits for interview
wear, and a general tendency to do things by the book.

One reassuring aspect of the changing trends in job hunting
is that being out of work is no longer the disgrace it used to
be. Layoffs, politically-motivated dismissals, and an increasingly tight job market mean that some of the business world's
best people have lost their jobs in recent years. Recruiters
agree that it's better to be employed while looking for a new
job, but being unemployed is no longer a stigma.

It is always fashionable to know exactly what you want to
do with your working life, as well as how, when and where
you want to do it. "It's very childlike to go into an interview

with an attitude that says 'tell me what to do with my life,' "
explains one personnel executive. "I think of knowing what
you want as career maturity."

Being a specialist with business-school credentials (particularly an MBA) is fashionable, but liberal arts majors should
not lose hope. "People who have gone to business school have
gotten strictly information-based educations," points out a
bank vice president who recruits fiduciary and staff department professionals. "The information they've learned will be
out of date in ten years. But people with liberal arts backgrounds have been educated in the ability to learn how to go
out and acquire more knowledge. If you've demonstrated the
ability to get a B + in history, you probably can learn banking
as well."

JOB HUNTING IS HARD WORK

Whether you're collecting unemployment checks or taking
home a tidy salary from a job that's begun to bore you, looking
for a new job is not going to be easy. Chances are you will
be rejected more than once, and that experience alone can
make you feel like giving up.

A support system is important. "Job hunting is a very lonely
process," agrees Manhattan-based career counselor Dr. James
F. Malone. "It takes a long time and it's demoralizing. You're
going to need someone to talk to." If you can afford it, an
initial consultation with a professional job counselor can be
good for general guidance and motivation. Later, you may
want to make a point of setting up special social occasions to
commiserate with other job seekers. When it seems as though
you'll never find the right job, knowing that other people feel
the same way can help.

Another good morale booster is to remember that you're a
competent, useful human being. Prove this to yourself by
doing something you know you do well. If it's working with
figures, catch up on the home accounts. If it's public speaking,
give a talk to your civic group. If it's cooking, make a soufflé.

The experience of having done a good job will help you get through the hard times.

Even if you're not planning to leave your employer for a long time, you should have a job hunting game plan. "Everyone should have an updated résumé ready and be in touch with headhunters in their field," urges Anne Sweeney, press relations manager for Inter-Continental Hotels, who was laid off from her previous job two weeks after notification that she was going to be promoted. If you suddenly find yourself being asked to clean out your desk, leave the job with dignity. Co-workers don't forget tantrums, word gets around, and bitterness is an ineffective interviewing style.

WAITING BY THE PHONE

As your job search gets underway, get organized. Max Peace, a corporate banking officer, recommends a system of index cards, alphabetically arranged and double-filed under both the name of the company and your contact there. He also advises that you "note the date of the interview, when there is one, and the major points that were brought out. Then keep the cards on your desk near the phone, so you can refer to them when that interviewer calls. It's tedious, but it's absolutely necessary, even if you have a great memory."

Perhaps the ultimate job-hunting secret is the one that public relations account executive Bruce Haxthausen reveals: "Patience, patience, and patience." You may find a great job in three weeks, but the time period most often mentioned by job hunters is one year.

Yes, some people just seem to walk into great job offers. But the chances are good that those people were making contacts and building credentials for years, consciously or not, getting ready for the right job to come along.

Opportunity favors the prepared job hunter. Twenty-one steps from now (or even sooner, if you've been doing some preparation all along), you can be one.

1

Focus on Your Job Goal

Why: You'll be more successful at a job you love and do well. And employers will count you out if they aren't convinced you want this particular job more than any other in the history of the world.

Time: 30 minutes a day of self-assessment for as long as it takes to establish your goal

If you won first prize at the science fair when you were eight, made straight A's while earning your Master's in Biochemistry, wake up every morning just itching to get at those test tubes and have found corporate research and development everything you hoped for in a career, skip this section.

But if you're working in quality control because it was the only entry-level job you could find after graduation, or if you went into law to please your parents, and the joy of working isn't living up to your expectations, it might be time for serious self-assessment.

Being unhappy in your current job, however, doesn't always call for a major career change. Don't switch occupations for the wrong reasons:

- *Because you can't stand one aspect of your job.* No career is perfect. Movie stars have to wake up at the crack of dawn when filming. Rural newspaper editors

1

have to cope with pressure from the townspeople. Trial lawyers have to deal with negative people all day.

- *Because you're sick and tired of office politics.* There's no escaping bureaucracy and favoritism. It's just a matter of finding the form you're least uncomfortable with and/or learning to enjoy the game.
- *Because your boss thinks you're no good at this.* Don't let one person convince you that you're unsuited to a certain career or don't perform a particular task well. The working world is made up of many tastes, opinions and work styles. Award-winning advertising executive Shirley Polykoff was turned down for a job on an early Clairol campaign, but later she went on to write successful slogans such as: "Is it true blondes have more fun?" and "Does she or doesn't she? Only her hairdresser knows for sure."

In cases like those above, a simple job change is probably the best answer. However, other situations may call for a more dramatic move.

7 GOOD REASONS TO SWITCH CAREERS

1. You like what you're doing, but would like to do it in a field that offers more money, prestige, security or all three.
2. You like what you're doing, but it's a dead-end occupation, or one that's expected to have limited opportunities in the years ahead.
3. You've always felt you'd love being a doctor, artist, salesperson, TV director or whatever. And you don't want to kick yourself at age 80 for never having tried.
4. You wake up every morning in mortal dread of going to work (but only if it's the work you dread, rather than a specific boss or co-worker).
5. You never look forward to any aspect of your work.
6. You never feel proud of your work.

7. You've just finished school and have no idea how your education and skills fit into the business world.

GETTING PROFESSIONAL GUIDANCE

Richard Flagg's situation fell under category number seven. He'd received a master's from Harvard in counseling/consulting/psychology, and came to New York City with no specific career goal in mind. Without a Ph.D., he couldn't go into private practice, but the idea of most corporate jobs left him cold.

"Most work really doesn't matter," Flagg explained. What he really wanted was a job in which he could do good for humanity, like his friend who works for the Helen Keller Foundation implementing self-help programs for the blind in Third World nations. Very few jobs like that were listed in the classified ads section.

After more than a year in the city, Flagg took a friend's recommendation and began to see a private career counselor. After meeting with her two to three times a week for five months, paying a monthly fee of $200, he emerged with a decision. Now he's ready to mount a serious campaign aimed at a job in human resources development.

"I'm aware now that I love being a coach," he explains. "Teaching per se gets very repetitive, but coaching people— giving them specific advice for specific situations—is a really satisfying way to live your life."

In human resources development, he'll have a chance to put people's tastes, talents, skills and experience to best use— possibly matching people to jobs they'll enjoy more than their present ones. "Everybody I know works because they have to," he points out. "It would be nice to be the person who makes a difference in helping them find the right work."

Flagg came to his realization in sessions similar to those with a psychiatrist, but focused on present-day realities. The career counselor gave him written assignments to aid self-evaluation, had him send for academic transcripts all the way back to grade school and even examined his leisure-time activities to help analyze his tastes.

"All play is rehearsing for work," Flagg notes. "You see it in nature. A kitten playing with string is training to catch things with her paws, because her future career is to be a good hunter." So it stands to reason that people's hobbies can reveal the type of work they'd like to be doing. Crossword puzzle fanatics often make good editors, but devoted squash players shouldn't be stuck behind a desk.

Career counselors sometimes send their clients to testing facilities for evaluation and career/aptitude matching, but for Flagg it wasn't necessary. His present counseling sessions concentrate on résumé writing, planning specific moves (such as signing up for a job-related course and joining a professional association) and rehearsing interviews by role-playing. Some clients, reluctant to make those important phone calls to personnel agencies or prospective employers, use session time to telephone from the counselor's office.

The Bad Guys

The counseling process has been known to change people's lives, but job hunters should beware of unscrupulous counseling services. "Most of the bad guys ask you to sign a contract up front for several thousand dollars," warns one independent counselor. "It's their job to convince you that just about everything is wrong with you, from your résumé to the way you part your hair. That way they can get you to sign up for the entire program, even if you really need help in only one or two areas."

Some services "guarantee" they'll find you work as well. Sharon Atkinson, attracted by the ads of a counseling organization in a leading newspaper, went for an interview, and was further impressed by the modern penthouse offices.

She wanted to work in Paris, but wasn't sure what kind of job she'd be able to find there. Admitting that her French wasn't perfect, she pointed out that she always had an aptitude for languages, and was currently studying French at night.

The counselor shook his head, then began to list all of her professional shortcomings as well as the barriers that stood between her and an overseas job. It would be a particularly difficult assignment for them, he explained, but for $4,000 they could probably assure her of something. "It's too bad your French isn't fluent like mine," the counselor said and proceeded to recite a few sentences *en Français.*

By that time Atkinson was so demoralized she was prepared to sign on the dotted line. But the man's errors in French grammar and pronunciation were obvious and cost him his credibility. Sharon Atkinson left the office, never went back and later learned that she'd been the victim of the group's usual method. If Truffaut had come to them for counseling, they would have told him that he'd never work in France without their costly help.

Not all counseling organizations are rip-offs, of course. If you've been fired or laid off, your former employer may provide you with the services of an outplacement agency. Because their services are free to you, take advantage of those that might be beneficial. Many outplacement agencies are also highly reputable executive search firms and can be good contacts.

DO-IT-YOURSELF EVALUATION

To help you choose a new occupation, it's important to know exactly which aspects of your present work situation please and displease you. And you may be able to analyze those areas without seeking professional help. Answering the following questions—on paper—can be a good start.

1. What three responsibilities in your current job do you enjoy most?
2. What three parts of your current job would you give a million dollars never to do again?
3. What three things do you miss most about past jobs?
4. What five work-related tasks do people compliment you about most?
5. What five tasks unrelated to your work do people compliment you about most?

To delve more deeply into your values and into the kinds of activities you really enjoy, try these exercises:

1. List 15 things you like to do. Then find the patterns (are they done alone or with people, are they free or costly, etc.?).
2. Describe your idea of an ideal work day, in detail, from awakening to bedtime. (You can live anywhere in the world, have any amount of money and spend that day with anyone you choose.)
3. If you could choose to live five completely separate lives, whose would they be? (King of England, movie sex symbol, world traveler, sculptor, housewife, etc.).

STICKING TO YOUR GUNS

Everyone has a variety of talents and interests and could be happy in a number of different careers. But in order to get a job, you need to be specific. Your task is to convince each and every interviewer that *this* is the one job you want.

Carolyn Hardy learned that lesson the hard way. Always fascinated by the advertising world, she had enjoyed writing for student newspapers and felt she'd make a good copywriter. When she managed to get a courtesy interview at a top agency, the copywriter looked at her résumé and said, "Well, you've never done any ad copy, but you have this general business experience. If you're interested in advertising, I think you'd be better off in account work."

Disappointed that a real professional didn't envision her as a creative genius, but eager to work in the glamorous advertising business, Hardy responded that she'd certainly be interested in looking into it. The copywriter set up an interview with an account executive at the same agency.

When the account executive saw her journalism degree and student reporting experience on her résumé, he asked if she'd ever considered going into copywriting instead. Relieved that this man recognized her true talents, she replied honestly, "Yes, but they sent me to you instead."

Carolyn Hardy was not offered a job in either area. Nor was she given a lead or recommendation by either interviewer. When reporting the incident to her friends, she was exasperated. "These people don't know what kind of experience they're looking for," she said. "Either that, or they were both just trying to get rid of me."

Years passed before Hardy realized that probably she had been subjected to a simple test and had failed. The copywriter-interviewer had wanted her to prove her sincerity and her serious interest in the field. It's a common interviewing technique.

Recruiters can be even more devious. "We've sent MBAs to banks for loan officers' jobs," recalls Linda Kline, head of Kline-McKay, a New York executive search firm. "At the end of an interview, the recruiter would say, 'Well, Joe, you've sat here talking about being a lending officer, but I'm not really sure I see you in that. If you had your choice to be anything else in the bank, what would you really like to do?' Some candidates think this guy is really interested in them, and they answer, 'Well, I'd really like to be in Personnel.' The recruiter says he'll keep Joe in mind when anything opens up. But after that candidate leaves the office, he makes a note—'Doesn't know what he wants to do'—and drops his résumé into a wastebasket."

According to Kline, the job candidate could have said, "I'm

very interested in this specific program. I'm really sorry you
don't see me as good for it, because it's what I'm really interested in. But if you see me as particularly suited for something else, I'd like to hear about it." The ball is back in the
recruiter's court.

Before you even consider going to an interview, know your
career goal and stick to it. Why should an employer believe
you'll stay on the job and learn, grow and be productive, if
you can't stand by a simple decision for the length of an interview?

Research the Job Market

Why: **Getting hired, and staying employed in the years ahead, will be easier if you're in a field that's expected to grow.**

Time: **Three or four 15-minute sessions**

Astronomers will have a rough time job-hunting this year. So will bookbinders, postal clerks, college teachers and merchant marines.

Once you've given careful thought to what you enjoy doing, what you do best and how you want to spend working days for the rest of your life, one important question remains. Does your ideal career exist in the current job market, and how easy will it be to get hired?

If all your talents and preferences add up to a career as a high school English teacher, don't expect to step into a great job overnight. The number of teaching jobs has been declining since the U.S. birth rate started dropping back in the mid-1960s. Even if the current baby boom continues and leads to a teacher shortage in the future, all of the unemployed teachers and former education majors who never got a chance to set foot in a classroom are already in line ahead of you.

If the job market looks tight for your chosen profession, you may want to analyze your love for it more closely. Is working with children the part of teaching that appeals to you most? Then consider training to become a health-care therapist and specialize in working with youngsters. Or is it the actual process of educating people that gives you satisfaction? Then consider a corporate job in training. You might work in personnel, teaching new employees about the company and the industry, or a job in sales training, educating customers about the use of computers or some other product line.

HOW MANY PEOPLE WANT THAT GLAMOUR JOB?

Part of understanding the job market is knowing the number of new jobs expected to be created in the years ahead. But it's equally important to be aware of the number of people trying to get those new jobs.

Maybe you're perfectly suited to a career as a television newscaster, and nothing would make you happier. A quick glance at the figures from the Bureau of Labor Statistics reveals that you've chosen a growing occupation. As cable TV expands, the amount of programming grows, the number of news/information shows increases and the number of newscaster's jobs should skyrocket. But watch out for the competition. Broadcasting is a visible and glamorous career, and almost anyone would be glad to trade occupational places with Barbara Walters.

This is not to say you should give up your dream. But if you decide to pursue a slow-growing or highly competitive career, be prepared. There are sacrifices, compromises and possible periods of unemployment ahead. Be ready with an alternative plan for paying the rent when times are bad, and be prepared to use every trick in the book (this one) to job-hunt like a predator.

On the bright side, knowing about the job market can help you in unexpected ways. Commercial artists face a very competitive market, for instance. But if you know that banking and insurance are growing industries, you can head off the competition by taking your portfolio to employers and clients in those fields. Marketing jobs are expected to grow at an average pace in the coming years, but what you're marketing makes a difference. If you apply for a job as brand manager for a computer products firm, your prospects are better than if you send your résumé to an auto manufacturer or a steel company. If you want to get into public relations (a fast-growing field, although affected by dips in the economy), your chances are better of landing an entry-level spot in a hospital's PR department than in the public affairs office of a state university where budgets are extra-tight.

If you're looking for a secretarial or entry-level management job, why waste your time calling and sending résumés to every company in town? You can focus your search on one or two industries, and slant your experience to show your interest in those areas. This makes job-hunting easier.

5 FAST-GROWING FIELDS WHERE YOU MIGHT FIND A JOB

1. Health Care

You don't have to be a doctor, nurse or technologist to be a part of the fastest-growing field of the decade. Hospitals, clinics, nursing homes and health maintenance organizations (HMOs) need the same kind of specialists any business requires: computer programmers, personnel interviewers, public relations writers, purchasing agents, secretaries and the like. This is a "hot" field because our population is growing older and increasingly health-conscious. And the widespread availability of medical insurance makes it easier for everyone to see a doctor and pay the bills.

2. Computers

If it seems that half the people you know have quit their old jobs to go into the computer business, that's only a slight exaggeration. The number of jobs for programmers and systems analysts is expected to grow dramatically between now and 1990, but the number of people trained to do those jobs has grown even more dramatically. Unless your heart and mind are set on programming, it may be wiser to get computer training, then use it in another occupation.

Being a computer expert makes you infinitely more marketable in every industry from banking to toymaking. The insurance industry is looking for claim representatives and underwriters who know data processing as well. Secretaries who can handle a word processor find jobs more easily than their uncomputerized counterparts. Even auto mechanics are using computers now to diagnose a car's ailing transmission.

The computer companies themselves are growing by leaps and bounds. And, like any other kind of industry, they need people in marketing, sales, personnel, accounting, etc.

3. Travel

Yes, travel. Several major U.S. airlines may be experiencing hard times, but by no means is this a dying industry. Some airlines are making money, particularly the regional carriers sprouting up everywhere, and the number of travel agents' jobs in the U.S. is expected to increase by at least 50 percent in the next few years.

And why not? Our older population, which is increasing, includes many with the leisure time and the retirement benefits to travel. Corporations are giving us all longer vacations. Foreign visitors flock to the U.S., and someone has to organize their tours. And business travel goes on, no matter what the state of the economy.

Airlines, travel agencies and hotels hire a variety of specialists and support personnel, and many corporations have their own travel departments. One important and growing specialty is incentive travel: company-financed trips organized to reward outstanding employees or suppliers.

4. Insurance

In the 1960s the biggest portion of our population was under age 25, and didn't own very much worth insuring. Now the post-World War II baby boom generation is well into adulthood, facing family and financial responsibilities. They are why the insurance industry is growing, and is expected to grow even faster in the years ahead.

Job prospects for actuaries, claim representatives and underwriters look bright in the years ahead. But every kind of job—from receptionist to corporate attorney—is available in insurance companies. Some growing specialties worth looking into include dental, prepaid legal, kidnap, product liability, medical malpractice and workers' compensation coverage.

5. Banking

Banking is a lot like insurance; its growth reflects the security-consciousness of our maturing population. And all those 24-hour automatic tellers that even accept the monthly payment on your bank charge cards are another indication of the industry's changing priorities and new array of services.

Although conservative, banks are excellent places to build a career: pleasant working conditions, topnotch benefits and job opportunities at every level from clerk and teller to top management. Almost every city and town in America has at least one bank branch, but the greatest number of banking jobs are in heavily populated states like New York, California, Illinois, Pennsylvania and Texas.

FACTORS THAT CREATE JOBS

The introduction of a new job market or the growth of an old one is usually related to important factors in society. The list below provides some examples of the social cause and its

job-related effect. Understanding these shifts can help you do
your own job-market analysis.

Older population	Doctor, nurse, health care technologist, health care therapist, geriatric specialist in many areas, hospital and nursing home administrator or employee
Maturing "baby boom" generation	Insurance professions (actuary, claim rep, underwriter), banking professions, real estate agent or broker
Economic hard times	Accountant, bankruptcy lawyer, collection worker, purchasing agent, economist, repair professions
The energy crisis	Geologist, geophysicist, petroleum engineer, ceramic engineer, metallurgical engineer, mining engineer, engineering technician
Corporate trends	Public relations, marketing research, personnel
Technology	Computer programmer, systems analyst, computer service technician, business machine repairer
Women in the work force	Restaurant occupations (including chef), floral designer, retail sales occupations, secretary

10 FAST-GROWING CAREER FIELDS THAT NEED WOMEN

	Percentage of women in work force
Engineering	4%
Architect	4%
Auto Sales	Less than 1%
Airplane Pilot	1%
Construction Occupations	Less than 1%–4%
TV/Radio Service	4%
Business Machine Repair	4%
Dentist	5%
FBI Agent	5%
Optometrist	5%

GETTING THE LOCAL PERSPECTIVE

Most job-market trends are nationwide, but there may be specific opportunities in your hometown or in a city you hope to move to. One way to find out is to read the want ads in your local Sunday newspaper—from A to Z. If Brookwood Hospital has placed ads for accountants and physical therapists, that can be important for you—even if your goal is a job in data processing. That hospital may be expanding in other areas too, and you'll be a step ahead of the competition by making contact now.

A more personal way to analyze the local job market is to draw up a list of your friends and acquaintances. Where are they working? Where have you heard of growth (or layoffs)? Where have people you know found new jobs in the past year?

If you want to know about a specific career field in your geographical area, write or call the Department of Labor in your state's capital city. They issue local labor-market reports on hundreds of occupations.

For more information: *90 Most Promising Careers For The 80s*
By Anita Gates (Monarch Press, 1982)

Choose Your Employer

Why: **Where you work and who you work with are just as important to job satisfaction as what you do all day.**

Time: **30 minutes of serious thought**

Neville Blount arrives at his office building a little after 9:30 AM, takes the elevator to 35 and emerges into an atmosphere of plush red carpet and oak-paneled walls. He nods hello to the receptionist (whose name he is almost sure is Evelyn), inserts his computerized ID card into a machine on the wall and is buzzed into the office area. The coffee wagon will pass his office in exactly five minutes. He has just ridden on the elevator with his company's chairman of the board, but didn't recognize him. Blount has never seen a photo of the man.

Eric Weaver gets to his office at 8:55 AM. The receptionist, an aspiring manager named Lisa who occasionally helps run focus groups, buzzes him into the front door of the small suite of offices. They talk about an upcoming meeting while Weaver pours himself a cup of coffee from the machine in the Xerox room. The company president passes by and compliments Weaver on a report he submitted the day before.

Both men are staff accountants in a large city.

Deciding what you want to do for a living is the most important step in setting your career goal. But deciding where you want to do it means thinking about working relationships, job atmosphere and the kind of experience you'll get.

Small or Large?

Big companies have their problems. Working there tends to involve you in bureaucracy; you'll probably have to fill out a form and get it approved by two people just to order a new stapler. The workings of corporate politics tend to be more complex in large companies. The atmosphere is usually more formal than in small organizations. For better or worse, your job there will tend to be highly specialized. For example, one staff artist will work exclusively on shelf talkers while another will be assigned only to package design.

But working for a big company has its advantages: you have more clout; you're always representing one of the biggest accounts around; and you have the prestige that comes from being associated with a known quantity. When you go job hunting later, many people will assume you're good at what you do if you've worked for a big company like Exxon or Bristol-Myers. And large companies usually offer more comprehensive benefits. Your medical coverage, savings plan and tuition refund program can make up for a less than generous salary increase.

Working for a small company has its pros and cons as well. You may have less prestige in some circles, less clout with clients or suppliers and a less impressive benefits package. In some areas, your risk of being laid off—if the company should lose one important account—is much greater than at a big company.

But you're more likely to gain broad, varied experience in your field. If you're great at what you do, the president is sure to know about it. You're more likely to find an informal, we're-all-in-this-together atmosphere (although office politics can be deadly) and red tape is virtually nonexistent.

Profit or Nonprofit?

Choose carefully when deciding whether you'll work for a profit or nonprofit employer. Switching from one to the other can be tough.

Education, government, hospitals, associations and other nonprofit sectors of the economy have been given something of an inferiority complex by big business. The goals and methods of profit and nonprofit companies may be much the same, but popular opinion has it that their mentalities are not. People often choose the corporate world because they consider anything else less than the "real business world"—and believe that the profit motive is where the action is.

Others choose nonprofit employers because they're offended by the idea of spending their lives at companies where the ultimate spiritual goal is the sale of industrial plastics or oven cleaner. In the nonprofit sector, no matter what the work may be, it's for a good cause: perhaps an end to environmental pollution, or the higher education of America's youth.

Keep in mind, however, that you can do good while employed by a conglomerate. Successful companies will often pour money into cultural and educational endeavors, and hire people to coordinate the projects.

After you've thought about these important decisions, find out which employers in your area fit the bill. Use library reference books like the *Standard & Poors Register of Corporations* to make a list of prospects. Use the Yellow Pages to find complete listings of every market research firm, advertising agency, department store, hospital and hotel in town. Ask people in your field which local company they consider most prestigious, and where you can get the best experience for the next career move.

You'll probably find two or three companies that seem to be ideal places to work. While you can't limit your job hunt to them, you can focus your search. Approach those companies first and in each let someone know how strongly you feel about working there someday. If it doesn't happen this time, you've made an important contact for the next job search.

Rewrite Your Résumé

Why: **Although it can't work magic, an impressive résumé tells employers a lot about you.**

Time: **Two or three 30-minute writing sessions**

Executives who hire new employees can be smug about their ability to pick and choose. "You know, we received more than 400 résumés for this job," one will say, "and picked six people to interview." (Implication: consider yourself lucky to be one of them.)

However, you're no longer impressed when a friend mentions an opening in her own department: "We put one ad in the Sunday paper for Ruth's job and got 700 résumés. Of course, half the people weren't at all qualified—and choosing from the other half was tough."

In a job market like that it's hard to get noticed. Perhaps that's why well-meaning career advisors have suggested devices such as brightly-colored stationery or professionally-set type. It's certainly why so many books have been written on résumés, and why entire companies have sprung up, claiming to have the secret for writing a magic résumé. You can learn from them, but don't expect miracles. Résumés don't get jobs; people do.

However, there are good résumés and bad ones. And even if a good one can't assure you of getting an interview, it's your most important asset once you reach that stage.

It's crucial to keep in mind that there are fashions in résumés. Right now there's a return to traditionalism in all aspects of job-hunting, and your résumé should reflect it.

- *Stay away from the functional résumé* (unless you have no business experience at all). "I'm suspicious of them," admits one personnel executive. "My first reaction is to assume the person is a secretary, or she wouldn't have to divide her experience up that way." The functional résumé organizes experience by category (administrative experience, sales experience, etc.) rather than by employer and year.
- *Don't get carried away with million-dollar accomplishments.* Rather than listing duties and responsibilities, a current trend in résumés is to impress recruiters with the problems you've solved, particularly in dollars-and-cents terms. "Implemented new distribution system that saved the company $500,000 in the first year." This was a great listing for the first 500,000 people who used it. Now it makes most recruiters yawn.

   If you won second prize with a company-wide money-saving suggestion, that's certainly worth noting. And mentioning the size of your budget or annual sales of the brands you were responsible for can substantiate the message in your résumé, but don't rely on it to explain who you are. One of the functions of a résumé is to make you stand out from the crowd. But following job-hunting fads can do just the opposite.
- *Don't spend a fortune on your résumé.* An elegant typesetting job with bold-face headlines and italics for the subheads just tells recruiters that you're desperate—or you're mailing this work of art to every employer in the continental U.S. Your résumé should be typed, error-free and single-spaced, on plain white or beige paper. Have it offset-printed at a neighborhood copy center for about $5 per hundred.
- *Do use the traditional format* (shown on following page). It's professional-looking, neat and easy to read. This is the old-fashioned chronological résumé, and it proves you have nothing to hide. For most people, a

1-page résumé is sufficient (please note that the résumé on pages 22–23 would fit easily into a 1-page format). But if you have years of business experience, up to 2½ pages is acceptable.

- *Show logical progression.* "A résumé should say to the recruiter, 'Here's what I've done and here's why I did it,'" explains a New York executive. In Lee Strickland's hypothetical résumé, early work for health-care clients is mentioned in order to show an ongoing interest and experience in that field. In fact, Strickland may have worked for more fashion clients than for any other specialty, but that's not the type of work he/she is looking for now.

- *Avoid technical jargon* (especially when looking outside your current field). One airline executive noted on her résumé a project she'd done at LAX—airline shorthand for the Los Angeles airport. Many nonspecialist recruiters thought this woman had been in the travel business so long she'd lost the ability to think any other way.

Ready, Set, Write

Now start thinking creatively about making your résumé what some job counselors refer to as "a picture of you in words."

- *Pretend you're writing a brochure about yourself.* If you were trying to impress someone who'd never heard of Meryl Streep, you wouldn't begin by saying "She has nine years acting experience" or naming her college degrees. To convey who Streep is, you'd have to start with "Two-time Academy Award winning actress for her performances in *Sophie's Choice* and *Kramer Vs. Kramer.*"

  Try to think about yourself in the same way. What headlines, catchy phrases and pictures would you use on a poster advertising your own importance? Make notes about them, then translate them into business language and the résumé format.

THE TRADITIONAL RESUME

Don't be bound by this basic format, only guided by it.

LEE STRICKLAND   <u>ART DIRECTOR</u>
299 South Hawthorne Road
Winston-Salem, NC 27103
Home (919) 555-2287
Office (919) 555-6350

<u>WORK EXPERIENCE</u>

1981-present   MARSTON MEDICAL
                                  COMMUNICATIONS
                                  Art Director

                                  Complete art direction
                                  responsibility for two bimonthly
                                  medical trade journals with a total
                                  circulation of 1.5 million.
                                  Coordinate all photo sessions, plan
                                  and supervise implementation of
                                  all editorial layout and type
                                  specification. Hire freelance
                                  photographers, illustrators and
                                  mechanicals artists on a regular
                                  basis. Supervise two staff artists.

1976–81   MIDLANDS BANK
                                  Art Editor

                                  Handled all layout, type
                                  specification, photo sizing and
                                  production supervision of two
                                  internal publications plus special
                                  design projects. Redesigned
                                  company newsletter.

1974–76   CAPRICORN GRAPHICS
                                  STUDIO
                                  Art Assistant

Handled design, layout and mechanicals projects for various clients, including St. Vincent's Hospital and the RGW pharmacy chain. Formats included brochures, flyers, newspaper ads and convention programs

FREELANCE   OAK STREET DENTAL CLINIC

Designed brochure and newspaper ads.

STYLES & CULVER FASHION SHOPS

Designed corporate letterhead, flyers and newspaper ads.

EDUCATION   B.F.A., University of Alabama, 1974

AWARDS   North Carolina Business Communicators "Best Two-Color Newsletter Design," 1979

PERSONAL   Born March 31, 1952
Married, two children
Excellent health

PORTFOLIO
AND REFERENCES   Available on request

- *Put the impressive facts first.* Feel free to rearrange what some people consider the correct order of a résumé. If you graduated summa cum laude from Harvard two years ago, put Education at the top of page one. If you once won the Pulitzer Prize, or even if you've taken home an impressive string of minor awards for your package design or sales campaigns, put Professional Honors before Work Experience. If you helped design Lady Diana's wedding dress, everything else in your fashion career is now secondary. Summarize your experience in a few sentences on page one, and put that royal project first.

- *Feel free to add categories.* If you graduated 11th in a class of 508, add a note about class standing to your Education section. Add a Skills and Abilities category if you type 95 words per minute, have mastered a computer language, speak fluent Hebrew or can proofread faster than a speeding bullet. Add International Travel if you've done more than your share. Add Media Appearances if you've talked about a business-related subject on *Donahue*—or just on a local radio show.

- *Look at friends' and co-workers' résumés.* Not because they have the secret formula, but because it's important to see how other people in your job field describe duties similar to yours. What language have they used that you feel make positive impressions? Negative ones?

- *Impress the reader with what you've done.* After you've made a list of your employers, job titles and dates of employment (most recent job first), it's time to explain what it is people have been paying you for doing all these years. To take a fresh look at your own qualifications and experiences, try these written exercises:

1. List ten responsibilities or projects you've had on each of your jobs. Put a star by the ones you enjoyed most, or feel will impress employers most favorably.
2. List five skills you feel were developed most during each job you've had.
3. Make the same two lists—responsibilities and skills—for high school extracurricular activities, college activities and summer jobs.

Use these lists to describe your work and talents in résumé form. Hold on to them until it's time to rehearse the job interview.

- *Do use all those action verbs.* One résumé trend hasn't lost its punch. For variety and impact, be sure to describe your work in dynamic terms, like the verbs below.

Administered	Instituted
Analyzed	Investigated
Booked	Managed
Checked	Marketed
Collected	Minimized
Compiled	Monitored
Composed	Negotiated
Conducted	Obtained
Converted	Organized
Coordinated	Planned
Created	Prepared
Designed	Projected
Developed	Ran
Devised	Reduced
Directed	Reorganized
Enhanced	Reported
Ensured	Represented
Established	Researched
Evaluated	Reviewed
Examined	Revised
Formed	Secured
Gathered	Selected
Handled	Serviced
Headed	Strengthened
Hired	Supervised
Identified	Surveyed
Implemented	Taught
Improved	Tested
Increased	Trained

Just be sure that the verbs you choose are appropriate to both the action and the field in which you work.

- *Choose your references carefully.* The names of references are never listed on the résumé itself, but you must have them ready. Employers are looking for business people who will vouch for your reliability, professionalism and the quality of your work. Former employers are ideal, but associates, clients and other professional contacts are fine.

If the president of Standard Oil is an old family friend who thinks the world of you, list him. But don't try to impress employers with the high placement of your references at the cost of getting a lukewarm response. References should have good business credentials, but it's more important that they speak highly of you.

As soon as you decide you're serious about finding a new job, get in touch with at least three people you'd like to use as references. Ask their permission, then type their names, titles, companies, addresses and business telephone numbers on a sheet of paper separate from your résumé. When a company is serious about putting you on the payroll, you have the list ready to present to your prospective supervisor or the personnel department.

THE FUNCTIONAL RESUME

If you're a housewife returning to the work force after a long absence, a student with no business experience or a worker who's had only one job, the functional résumé may be your only answer. Be sure to combine it with a chronological listing of your employment, as shown on the facing page. Employers want to know where you've been all your life.

When you've written the first draft of your résumé, read it over and ask:

1. For the kind of job I want, what are employers looking for that they don't see on my résumé?

THE FUNCTIONAL RESUME

KIMBERLY DANIELS

Job Objective:
Position as editorial assistant with possible career advancement to editor.

History:

June 1983
B.A. in Journalism, University of Missouri

June–August 1982
MIDDLETOWN GAZETTE
Reporter/summer internship

July–August 1980
THE BURGER HUT, Middletown
Fulltime waitress

Work Experience:

Writing
Published more than a dozen straight news articles during internship with **MIDDLETOWN GAZETTE**, including coverage of Presidential visit to Shelby County.

Wrote an average of eight feature articles per month as Assistant Features Editor of The **BLUE AND WHITE** (student newspaper).

Editing
Edited 48-page college Panhellenic Manual, including complete responsibility for type specification, galley proofreading and coordination with art director, printer and sorority contributors.

Working knowledge of all editing and proofreading symbols.

Interviewing   Have interviewed college president,
                                various faculty members, student
                                leaders and visiting celebrities
                                (including Dr. Timothy Leary and
                                G. Gordon Liddy) for articles in
                                college newspaper.

General Business   Handled busy multi-line telephones
Experience   in newspaper office
                                (MIDDLETOWN GAZETTE).

                                Three months' experience with
                                word processing equipment.

                                Public contact experience during
                                summer job at local restaurant

Personal   150 West End Avenue
                                New York, NY 10023
                                (212) 555-9318
                                Single
                                Excellent health

References   Furnished on request.

---

2. What can I add that will prove I do have what they're
   looking for?

                                   or

3. What education, training, skills or experience do I
   need to fill in the gaps?

Steps 5 and 6 of this book offer some possibilities.

STEP 5

Take a Computer Course

Why: Computer knowledge is the one qualification employers in virtually every field ask for most. Credentials like this make you more marketable.

Time: 30 minutes or less to enroll. Three hours total to two hours per week for the course itself.

Programmers, systems analysts, managers of information systems and computer science majors or minors, skip to page 32, paragraph 2. The other job hunters, however, may want to take a lesson from Arthur Shaw's experience.

Shaw had a solid 12 years of experience in personnel interviewing when the computer revolution hit. Suddenly all the jobs seemed to be for technical recruiters—people to interview and screen data processing employees. And for the first time in his career, Shaw was having trouble switching jobs.

"We know you can handle this job, Arthur," he was told at one company, "but, in order to interview people for even the entry-level programming jobs, you have to know high-tech jargon and the right questions to ask these computer types. You and I both know you could pick it up on the job in a few weeks. But how am I going to explain hiring you when we're sitting on 100 résumés of people who already have the background?"

The difference between a recruiter and a technical recruiter may simply be a matter of understanding terms of the trade, but it holds a lot of people back. And announcing to the head of personnel that you're a fast learner rarely will get you hired. Reading up on a subject can teach you a lot, but it lacks a certain credibility on the job application. "9/83—Read two books about software" doesn't carry the same weight as "1983—Introductory and intermediate data processing seminars, New York University." With the latter, a personnel interviewer, agency or hiring manager can defend his or her choice in recommending you. "No, she hasn't hired data processing people before," they can say, "but she just spent a semester learning programming at NYU."

It works the same way for technical writers, technical salespeople and a variety of other relatively new job categories. Computer programming and operating knowledge can increase your chances of getting hired in almost any field—even when the job description doesn't call for it. "Find me a person who knows both the insurance business and computers," says a Connecticut insurance executive, "and I can guarantee they'll have no trouble finding a job."

Picking the Course

One school for continuing education describes its Introduction to Computer Programming and Data Processing course in these words:

> An introduction to what computers are and how they are used. Topics include types of computer systems, computer languages, flow charts, number systems, how to program a computer, types of computer instructions and typical applications. No prerequisites.

At the same school, you can move on to courses in Assembly Language Programming, COBOL, PASCAL, BASIC; Structured Programming; or Introduction to System Analysis and Design. Because most introductory courses will cover the material you need, your only decision is where to study.

- Take the same course a friend or associate has taken and been happy with.
- Ask a person who specializes in hiring computer personnel to name the best schools in your area.
- Call a computer company's local sales or personnel office and ask for a school recommendation.
- Ask a programmer or systems analyst where he studied, or where the people he works with learned about computers.
- If all else fails, pick a school by its overall reputation. It will look better on your résumé to have taken a course at UCLA than at Ralph's Incredible Technical Institute.

What if you sign up for a course and find you're not happy with it? Due to a shortage of qualified computer science teachers, this could happen at the best of schools. If it does, drop out immediately, get your money back (assuming the school has a refund policy) and try another course.

Paying the Bill

When it comes to tuition, higher education is costlier than ever. Now that the average private university charges almost $8000 per year, your bill for a full semester of classes in one course may be several hundred dollars. If you're currently employed and tuition refund is part of your benefits package, try to convince your immediate supervisor that a particular course will make you a more valuable employee. The company may pick up the tab that way. If not, the tuition is probably tax deductible.

There are some courses that are reasonably priced. Major universities have four- and five-session courses for $100 or

less. Adult education facilities like Network For Learning
have offered half-day seminars for less than $50. And in
overpriced New York City, a YWCA recently offered a two-
hour computer seminar for $15. Even if a short course doesn't
teach you everything you want to know, it's a start. It may
help you overcome your fear of high technology and whet
your appetite to learn more. Keep in mind that the few
hundred dollars you spend this year can lead to new earning
opportunities in the years ahead.

BACK-TO-SCHOOL ALTERNATIVES

Taking a computer course is not the only academic route
to career success. In this age of the specialist, anyone can
make himself more marketable—or fill in a gap in work experience—by taking a course or two at night.

If you're an experienced but out-of-work programmer who's
decided that banks make good employers, but you know
nothing about banking, sign up for an evening course in
banking procedures or financial analysis and learn the vocabulary of finance. Then add this credential to your résumé.
It will prove to a recruiter that you're serious about getting
into the field; it's also a good place to make professional contacts. Your teacher may be a banking professional by day (or
know many), and some of your fellow students may be bank
employees taking the course to qualify themselves for pro-
motions.

Perhaps you're an experienced legal assistant who has a
way with a word processor. But so do a lot of people, and
they're all competing with you for the field's best jobs. You
might want to learn Japanese, German, Spanish or French.
People may joke about language majors having no place in
today's job market, but bilingual employees are valued by
many industries that need legal help—from electronics to
fashion.

The right education and talents can turn you into a triple specialist. A Massachusetts man, with a master's in Nordic languages, took a journalism course and marketed his longtime interest in interior design. He now specializes in writing about Scandinavian castles for decorating magazines. No one else on staff can interview the royal owners in perfect Swedish.

At the very least, take a business-related seminar sponsored by a professional association in your field. Even major universities have become specific about teaching job skills to adults. You can sign up for Architectural Drafting, Marketing Law, Fashion Buying or Product Development Strategies right across the hall from classes in Michelangelo and the Italian Renaissance.

Work Free

Why: **Volunteer work doesn't have to mean rolling bandages. Volunteering in the career area of your choice is sometimes the only way to get the experience you need.**

Time: **As little as an hour or two per week**

Alison Garrett loved her editorial management job in a corporate public relations department, but it had turned into a dead end. If she ever expected to run a PR department or head her own agency, she needed strong publicity experience—not only writing and distributing releases, but organizing press conferences, developing long-range programs and making contact with newspaper and magazine editors.

Garrett had a good idea of how it was done, in part from the classroom (college courses and professional seminars), and in part from observing publicist co-workers. But she needed real experience, and her current employer was reluctant to provide it. A note on her annual performance review spelled it out: "Alison has expressed interest in working on product publicity, but her skills and personality do not seem suited to this kind of work. She will not be encouraged." Headhunters sought her out, but only for editorial jobs.

Then one Saturday she was having a facial. The skin care specialist announced that she'd soon be opening her own salon and hoped Garrett would continue to be a client. The woman mentioned an opening party for customers and the press, but complained that there was no budget for a PR representative. "I'll handle your publicity in return for a few free facials," Garrett volunteered—and a beautiful working relationship was born.

The salon found itself praised in *Vogue,* among other publications, and Garrett soon acquired four paying PR clients in the beauty industry. She left her full-time job, doubled her income the first year and no one ever asked what her first client had paid.

DO YOU NEED TO VOLUNTEER?

Working without pay works. When college students do it during the summer or part-time during the school year, it's called interning. And most employers regard it as real business experience, because some interns *are* salaried. In fact, many students stay on with their first employer and move up to responsible well-paying jobs.

The business world, however, has prejudices against adults who work without pay, so never list volunteer work—as such—on your résumé. If you're employed full-time and do volunteer work at night or on weekends, list it as "freelance" or "consulting" work along with whatever paid work of that kind you've done.

If an interviewer should ask about the money you earned "consulting," you may want to be evasive: "It varies according to the projects each month" is one way to handle the question. You're safe doing this. Many corporations won't reveal or confirm employees' salaries when called for reference; and it would be unusual for the supervisor at your volunteer job to reveal how much you were paid. Even if a call is made to the personnel department of a large company that you did some work for, and the person is told you were never on staff, that's fine. Paid freelancers and consultants aren't on the regular payroll, but work as contract labor—sending in bills at the end of the month like any supplier.

Working without pay can be a good idea if you need a certain kind of business experience in order to take the next step on the career ladder. It's also worthwhile if you need to become familiar with the day-to-day workings of a particular industry or specialty. But where should you volunteer to work?

- Small companies are easier to get into, and there's less red tape about hiring.
- Entrepreneurs starting new businesses almost always need help. Ask among your friends and, in large cities, read trade journals for new business announcements.
- Many nonprofit associations are accustomed to the idea of unpaid help. For credibility, choose one that uses both salaried and volunteer people.
- Don't choose a controversial cause. Developing a direct-mail marketing program for the Symbionese Liberation Army may have been great experience, but it's bound to turn off a recruiter or two. Sadly, some people still consider NOW a radical organization.
- Work for a professional association in your field to learn many aspects of the business. If you're trying to break into real estate, having answered phones for the National Association of Realtors would make a great reference.

OVERCOMING THE OBJECTIONS

Most people still think of volunteer work as something for bored housewives or restless teenagers. That's why your first offers to work without pay may be met with confusion or even firm refusals. Be prepared.

"If you're so great, why are you willing to work for nothing?" Explain that it is unusual, but your particular career goal requires learning a great deal about this specific area. Of course,

you won't be able to work without pay forever, but meanwhile this could be a mutually beneficial arrangement. You'll help out in whatever area the company needs work done, because the only way to really learn a business is to see how professionals handle its day-to-day realities.

"The only help we need around here is in doing the dirty work." Fine. You'll get the coffee, clean out the office supplies closet and deliver envelopes to clients in the pouring rain, as long as you get a little time to ask questions and try your hand at higher-level duties.

"I'd feel guilty about not paying you." If you run into this attitude, offer to barter. You'll design your hairdresser's promotional brochure in return for free haircuts.

"When will you find time?" If you're working full-time, you still have lunch hours, evenings, weekends and vacation days. When you're serious about getting ahead in your career, the sacrifice is worth it. Four hours a night plus Saturdays would add up to a 28-hour volunteer week.

What you're willing to do will depend on your career level at the moment. If you're 19 and just starting out, you can afford to take the staff's sandwich orders. But even if you're older and earning $75,000 a year as a senior VP, the work-for-free principle can be a good idea. Simply start your own business and discreetly arrange to give away your products or services to that first client—just to get established.

Polish Your Résumé

Why: That résumé is your most tangible job-hunting tool. And most hiring managers tend to interview from it.

Time: Two half-hour rewrite sessions

The first time Roger Kepke had to hire someone above secretarial level, he received 200 résumés—and conscientiously read each one. With great difficulty he picked out five job candidates and asked them in for interviews. In person none of the five seemed quite right.

He discussed it with a higher-level executive who suggested that he look for candidates with a particular work background. Kepke reread the remaining 195 résumés and selected five new candidates. Again, no one seemed to have all the right qualifications.

Eventually he filled the job by working with a personnel agency. Months later the new employee made a confession: His had been one of the original 200 résumés.

If it's all a roll of the dice, why devote two steps of your job search to creating the perfect résumé? "The answer is that a fabulous résumé won't automatically get you a job or even get you noticed," explains a New Jersey personnel director, "but a bad one is sure to work against you. No job hunter can afford to throw a résumé together. It takes a lot of thought and planning."

Executive search consultant Linda Kline points out that many hiring managers do interview candidates from their résumés. Many people in a position to hire aren't sure what to ask, so they look at your résumé for inspiration. The first step in controlling your interview—which means making it work in your favor—is to give the interviewer a résumé that will lead to the right questions.

"I'm always amazed when people come in for their first interviews and say, 'It's not on my résumé, but . . .' and then mention some special qualification," says a Manhattan employment agency owner. "If it's so important or terrific, why isn't it on paper?"

Give these questions serious thought. Why should ABC, General Electric or any company hire you for the job you want? What makes you better than the last person who held your current job? What do you do better than most other people? And how does the experience you have prove that? What in your experience helps you know about a field you may never have worked in full-time?

You can also make information known by beginning your résumé with a summary in paragraph form. In no more than three or four sentences, tell the recruiter who you are, or point out something about you that didn't quite fit into any other category.

If you're answering an ad to work for a nonprofit foundation that will study the effects of frequent travel on health, this wrap-up would be perfect.

> SUMMARY: Eight years' business experience, including three years with a travel agency and two years as a market research associate specializing in health-care research. Research topics have included jet lag and in-flight meal service. Have attended seminars on aviation health and safety.

This kind of information, designed to slant your experience toward the needs of a specific employer, can go into a cover letter or be part of a résumé tailor-made to suit each job. The higher your status in business, the more likely you are to need several résumés instead of just one. Keep your basic résumé on hand, however, and work from it when writing spin-offs.

BUT I DON'T NEED A RESUME

Everyone who works for pay, or wants to, should have an up-to-date résumé at all times. No one is too high or too low on the business ladder to escape this simple ritual.

Clerical workers may be asked to fill out lengthy applications with the same kind of information that usually appears on a résumé. But not every company follows that procedure, and you could end up in the hiring manager's office empty-handed.

"It makes a very bad impression when it happens," confirms Judy Eidsvaag, Director of Sales for Networld, Inc. "One secretarial candidate came in with no résumé at all, so I had to ask her where she'd worked and when, where she'd gone to school, all of it. And I had to sit there making my own notes about her." The woman in question was not asked back for a second interview.

On the other end of the scale, many executive search firms send a Candidate Profile Report instead of a résumé to the company looking for a new executive. "But we prefer a résumé to work from," agrees Gary Marshall, a vice president of Smyth Dawson Associates in Stamford, Connecticut.

Some job-hunting methodologists recommend sending out "broadcast letters" highlighting your accomplishments—unaccompanied by a résumé. Like many other job-hunting trends, this could be dramatically effective if no one else but you were doing it. However, this approach was popularized by career books more than a decade ago, and some recruiters are exasperated by the practice. Send a résumé.

Making It Perfect

Your résumé should be error-free. Ask a knowledgeable friend to proofread it for typing errors, misspellings and grammatical mistakes.

Don't be swayed by one friend's suggestions on improving the résumé itself, however. One person's brilliant idea is another's pet peeve. "I really hate to see those phrases like 'All-American family man and home owner' or résumés that say they're looking for jobs with a 'responsible, conservative U.S. company,'" admits a corporate recruiter. "Someone has told them that these are buzzwords, something to signal us that they're 'our kind of people.' But it turns me off completely and makes me wonder what they're hiding or really trying to say."

What if your résumé reveals a problem like constant job-hopping or a long stretch of unemployment? Most interviewers agree that it's best to be honest about the time you were out of work. Attitudes toward unemployment have changed drastically in recent years.

If you took a year off to travel, that's a perfectly acceptable decision (unless you show a history of doing this every three years). If you were in school, even part-time, list that to account for the gap. If you left work to marry and/or raise a family, you may want to mention that in your summary on the résumé's first page.

Job-hopping is more difficult to deal with. Some counselors suggest you simply omit some of your jobs. But if you expand the amount of time you were on other jobs to cover those years, you're very likely to get caught. Because so many people exaggerate on their résumés, many employers hire investigative agencies to check out applicants' stories.

Your best bet is to examine your career path so far, try to find some direction to it and try to convince the interviewer that all these experiences have led you to the long-term position you've always wanted—this one.

8

Get in Touch
With 20 People

Why: Seven out of ten jobs are filled by personal recommendation. It really is who you know, so get out there and mingle.

Time: Five minutes per phone call, 30 minutes or less per letter

Barbara Dyson has had seven secretaries, all of them properly screened, interviewed and hired at the Fortune 500 conglomerate for which she works. Yet only three of those seven got their jobs without special recommendations of a sort. Of the other four, one was a co-worker's younger sister fresh from business school; another, a temporary who did so well on her one-week assignment that she was asked to stay on; the third was first interviewed as a favor to a woman in personnel; and the fourth was the girlfriend of a man Barbara had met in group therapy.

Why do people always sound bitter when they say "You've got to know somebody to get ahead," or "It's who you know, not what you know"? It may be true that being named Hemingway or Du Pont has incredible advantages, but everyone has friends, relatives, co-workers and former teachers. When you're serious about your career, you come to realize that you've been making contacts all your life. It's up to you to use them.

CALL YOUR 10 FAVORITE PEOPLE

Even the people closest to you may not realize that you want and need their help in your quest for a new job."When I finally asked people for assistance, a lot of them looked surprised and said 'I just assumed you already had something lined up,' " recalls Bruce Haxthausen, a travel industry publicist. "You have to say to each and every person, 'I'm looking for a job.' You can't just assume they know that."

And if ten favorite people don't immediately come to mind, try making up your list by asking yourself these questions:

- Who were the last ten people I had lunch with?
- Who were the last ten people I saw socially? (Exclude your present boss and any of his or her immediate family.)
- If I were planning a dinner party, who are ten interesting friends I would invite? (In fact, why not give that dinner party and then bring up job hunting? Do individual follow-up later. People feel less responsibility to help when they're approached as a group.)

What you have to say to your friends is simple: "I'm starting a serious job-hunting campaign. This is what I'm looking for. Would you keep your eyes and ears open for me?"

This statement gives you a new visibility and places you in your friends' minds in a certain category. When they hear the words art director, purchasing agent, social worker or whatever your occupation happens to be, they'll think of you. Your career may not have been a big part of their image of you before.

Add a second question when contacting friends, so you can find out if they have contacts you don't know about. Let's say you've decided that you want your next job to be in a hospital, preferably General Hospital on Maple Street. Just ask, "Do you happen to know anyone who works at General Hospital?" "Do you know anyone at all who works in the health-care field?" You may be pleasantly surprised to find that someone close to you has a contact he never thought of passing along. And even if that contact is an orderly or the maternity ward receptionist, it's a foot in the door. One way or another, it could lead to a courtesy interview (see page 47).

WRITE TO 10 INFLUENTIAL PEOPLE YOU'VE LOST TOUCH WITH

Don't bother to call Bill Blass because you met him once and now you want to break into the fashion business. The secret is not to contact the ten most highly placed people you ever shook hands with, but to seek out people who know you well enough to recommend your work. Then find out what contacts they can offer. Some possibilities:

- A former boss who liked your work and with whom you parted on friendly terms
- A teacher who always gave you A's (preferably in courses related to your work)
- Three best friends from your first job; from your last job
- School friends who majored in the same subject you did and now live in the same city
- School friends who worked on extracurricular projects with you and now live in the same city
- Former clients you enjoyed dealing with
- Former company suppliers you enjoyed working with
- Friends of your parents, sibling or spouse who are active in the business world—or the particular field you're interested in.

The first rule is not to bother cultivating the professional friendships of people you dislike or disrespect. It probably won't work because your true feelings will show through. But more importantly, it's not necessary. All kinds of people make it to the top—some you'll despise and some you'll love. You'll find your work a lot more pleasant if you deal with the people whose company you enjoy and whose style you could easily emulate.

Whether you decide to reestablish contact with people by letter or phone is a matter of personal taste. Just be sure to make that list of ten people, and do get in touch.

Hello, It's Me Again

TV comedian Carol Burnett once did a skit in which she receives a surprise phone call from the boy she adored twenty years before in high school. He's in town and wants to see her. But when he arrives, it turns out he only wants to sell her life insurance.

Getting in touch with people after years of silence just to ask them for a favor can seem pretty callous, but it's a reality of the job market that people can sympathize with more than ever. And there are gracious ways to go about it.

> Dear Dr. Powell:
> I hope you'll remember me. I was a student in your environmental graphics seminar two years ago. I remember this course vividly, because it was a determining factor in my decision to make a career switch to visual merchandising.
> I'm going to be passing through Philadelphia on the 16th and wondered if you might have time for lunch or a cup of coffee between classes. I've taken some additional design courses while working part-time in New York and am now eager to tackle my first full-time job in the display field. I thought you might be able to offer some advice on the best places to look and how to go about it.
> In any event, it would be a pleasure to see you again. I'd love to hear if any of your current students have outdone our class on the midterm project. I'll give your office a call next week in the hope that we'll be able to arrange something.
> Best wishes,

Or, if the person you're writing to is more or less a peer:

Dear Brenda,
How are things going at Smith, Snyder and Duke? It
seems much longer than three years ago we were still
struggling assistants at Greene-Arnold. But it is, and I
know that because I was just updating my résumé and
was faced with the awful truth.
    Keep it under your hat, but I'm giving serious
thought to moving on to something new. Trying to
summarize my work at Greene-Arnold really brought
back those days and reminded me of those incredibly
unproductive lunches we used to have in the second
floor cafeteria.
    That's why I'm writing. It's been too long, and I'd
love to see you again. Maybe you can give me the
inside scoop on who's hiring, and on what it's like to
have made the switch to nonprofit. Lunch is on me—
for a change.
                                        See you soon?

MEETING WITH OLD FRIENDS

The nicest part about networking is that people really do
want to help, for practical reasons as well as humanitarian
ones. Why shouldn't the printing salesman you used to work
with want to see you ensconced in a great new job? You'll
probably throw a lot of work his way. And if your family doctor
recommends you for an assignment at the new cable TV station in town (the president is his golf partner), you just might
think of that same doctor when the evening news team wants
to interview a medical expert.
    Meeting with an old friend, a former teacher or a longtime
family associate is not an interview, but some of the same
rules apply. This is not the time for soulsearching, secret-

sharing or outward signs of despair. Be honest, but present yourself as confident and positive—even if you're worried that you may never work again. This person doesn't want to recommend a job candidate who is on the verge of a nervous breakdown.

If the person is not exclusively a professional acquaintance, feel free to talk about your personal life. And be sure to ask about the other person's work, family and current interests. Common courtesy requires very little effort.

In this kind of get-together, three questions are appropriate:

1. Will you let me know if you hear of anything in my field? A job I might be right for?
2. Could you possibly set up a meeting or interview with _____ ?
3. How can I repay the favor?

Be sure to keep in touch with anyone who's offered to help on your job search, and take the time to thank them for any leads or actual interviews they've been able to arrange. You might give the person a résumé at the meeting (so they'll have some idea of your background) or mail one later.

The Courtesy Interview

When your best friend has arranged for you to talk to his boss, a former co-worker has set up a meeting for you with her cousin, the director of R&D, you have what is sometimes disparagingly known as a courtesy interview. But don't take it lightly.

Your goal on this occasion is to make a new contact, a favorable impression and to be remembered. A courtesy interview may lead to nothing. But it may lead to another contact, an important piece of industry information or an as-yet-unadvertised job with the very person who says there aren't any jobs right now.

But leave that unspoken. Your stated goal is to learn more about this particular industry and to get this person's expert advice on what you should be doing to prepare for a good career in this field.

Whether you call or write to set up the courtesy interview is up to you. Your mutual acquaintance may even make the arrangements for you. Treat it as if it were the real thing, because it might turn out to be. Dress in your job-interview wardrobe, be punctual and rehearse possible questions and answers (see Step 16). And keep these thoughts in mind:

- *Be flattering.* Everyone wants to be wanted, so indicate to the interviewer that, although you know there are no jobs available at the moment, a job at this company working for him or her is your ultimate goal. Be prepared to give convincing reasons.
- *Have a purpose.* Be prepared with specific questions, rather than just asking the executive to tell you all about the industry. "What sort of skills and experience are you looking for when hiring people in my field? Which skills are hardest to find these days? What are the best schools for people in my field? Could you explain some of the technical terms I've heard? What professional association would you suggest I join?"
- *Make your points.* As part of your preparation, list three important points about yourself, and find a way to work them into the interview. For example, if you've organized community relations projects (even though it's not part of your job description), you might ask the interviewer whether others will consider that valuable experience.
- *Follow-up is crucial.* Do send a note thanking the executive for his or her time, possibly enclosing an updated résumé "to let you see how much your suggestions helped." Mention your mutual acquaintance as a reminder that you came personally recommended.

Because the courtesy interview is primarily an information-gathering process, you may want to ask the executive for permission to tape the session. If you get the OK, use a cassette recorder with a built-in mike, place it on the interviewer's desk, turn it on and forget about it. Later, you'll be able to take down perfect notes on the career advice you received. You'll also be able to evaluate your interview style and work on any problems you discover.

STEP 9

Join a Professional Association

Why: Where else will you find 100 career contacts in the same room at the same time?

Time: One lunch hour or cocktail hour per month

Bruce Haxthausen doesn't even belong to the American Society of Travel Agents (ASTA), but he probably owes his current position to networking within the group. It was at the ASTA convention that he ran into a former colleague and mentioned that he was now considering a full-time situation, instead of freelance assignments. Three months later, recommended by that co-worker, he received a call about a freelance job.

"I didn't bring a résumé and there was no formal interview," Haxthausen recalls. "In fact, the company president had hardly set eyes on me when he said, 'I hope you'll consider joining us.'" The freelance work became full-time work. It may have been Haxthausen's trade press experience that clinched the offer, but it was that personal contact at the trade convention that got things started.

If you feel you're too busy job hunting to bother with professional associations, you've missed the point. Or if you've joined a group for the prestige but never go to meetings, you aren't getting your money's worth.

PICKING THE RIGHT ASSOCIATION

Virtually every occupation in America has at least one professional association from the American Association for Respiratory Therapy to the Society of Petroleum Engineers. And most occupations offer a choice of several organizations, depending on your tastes and special interests.

If you're already in your chosen field, you probably know the right organizations. If not, just ask co-workers. You may be able to get your current employer to pick up the tab for your association dues. If you're told it's an unnecessary expense, write the check yourself. Look for an organization with the greatest number of meetings for the money. What you're paying for is the opportunity to meet people. Why pay $150 a year to belong to an organization that holds semi-annual meetings—no matter how prestigious—when a similar association may charge $75 dues and hold monthly gatherings?

Membership Is Not Enough

Now that you've joined, you can list the association's name at the end of your résumé. But your membership is a waste of money if you don't go to the meetings regularly, and make the most of those occasions.

- *Dress in your best business clothes.* Even if it's the annual Christmas party and you've taken the week off, look as though you've just come from the office.
- *Carry your business cards.* If you're unemployed, have your own cards printed listing yourself as a consultant, freelancer or whatever is appropriate. If you're a secretary hoping to move into management, have cards printed with the company name and department but no title.
- *Meet at least two new people at each gathering.* If you're uncomfortable mingling with strangers, cocktail-

party style, choose luncheon or dinner meetings. With one person on each side of you for an hour or two, you're forced to strike up a conversation.

- *Make yourself visible.* Another way to avoid the cocktail hour is to volunteer to take money or tickets or hand out nametags at the registration desk. Or volunteer to escort the guest speaker, who may not know anyone there and could turn out to be a good contact.
- *Be natural, but never negative.* These get-togethers have a social element that encourages everyone to let down their hair, but it's a mistake to gripe openly about mistreatment at your job or the ogre you work for. No one wants to rescue you from an awful situation; they want to steal great people from other employers.
- *Get to know your peers.* People at your own job level (or just above it) can be even better contacts than top executives. After all, your peers will leave their jobs and need to be replaced someday. They get calls from headhunters in your field asking for recommendations too.

Work on a Committee

The best way to get the attention of the top people in an association is to be an active, contributing member. After observing the group for a few meetings, volunteer to work on a committee. It's the perfect chance to show off your talents, willingness to work and dependability. Which committee? You can choose in several ways:

- *The one in which you can perform best.* The social committee, for instance, if you're a great organizer, or if your cousin is a caterer.
- *The one the president of AT&T works on.* A great way to meet the executive you want to impress.
- *The most visible one.* If you introduce the speaker or give a report at every meeting, people will soon know who you are.

- *The one where help is needed most.* To prove you're a team player.

Don't volunteer until you know you have the time and willingness to do a good job. The worst thing you can do is make a commitment and not come through. "Oh, I remember Kelly," they may say, "she's the one who offered to find experts on environmental issues for the seminar, and never even got back to us."

And what if you're a beginner in your career field and won't be accepted into association membership? In most cases, you can still attend the meetings as a guest or nonmember by paying a small admission fee. You'll be learning more about your new field, and at the same time you're making contacts.

Other Ways to Use Associations

Conventions can be important meeting places. Don't limit yourself to gatherings of people in your own profession; making contacts in related fields can be just as important. If you're a sales representative looking for a job in the beauty products industry, head for the NHCA (National Hairdressers and Cosmetologists Association) convention. You'll find executives from the major beauty products companies there, and very little competition for their attention. It's much easier to stand out here than if you attended a convention made up exclusively of sales executives.

Try to win awards. You can only do this by entering competitions, many of them sponsored by professional associations. On your résumé, it's evidence of your having done good work.

Accreditation is available thrugh many organizations. If you're an actuary or CPA, of course, the process is more formal and absolutely necessary in order to work. But other professional accreditations merely make good credentials. The Public Relations Society of America and Professional Secretaries International are just two of the organizations that offer certification programs as evidence that you know your craft.

Remember the Alumni

College years may or may not have been the best ones of your life, but college alumni are mysteriously loyal to each other. It may be status ("We Harvard men have to stick together") or something as obvious as old friendships and common interests. It may even be a sense of bonding in an alien environment. Knowing someone else who went the University of Mississippi means more in New York, for instance, than in Tupelo or Atlanta. Even business schools have alumni groups that can be valuable for networking.

Should you belong to other kinds of clubs? If you have the time, they can't hurt. Maybe the creative director of the ad agency you want to work for is a skydiver or an orchid enthusiast like you—but you'll have a better chance of meeting her at the Ad Council luncheon.

Read the Classified Ads— Between the Lines

Why: **Not only to answer them, but to discover who's hiring and what the employers in your field are looking for.**

Time: **A full hour over Sunday morning coffee**

Only one out of eight jobs is filled through classified ads, but that's no reason to ignore them. For one thing, it may be the only way to get the one job that was tailormade for you. For another, classified ads can be a gold mine of information about the job market, when you know how to analyze them properly.

WHAT ARE PEOPLE LOOKING FOR?

If you're making a career switch and don't know what kind of training you need, the local want ads can help you. In a recent Sunday edition of *The New York Times*, for instance, 23 ads for travel agents specifically mentioned knowledge of reservations systems. Of those, 19 called for SABRE, 3 for

Apollo and one for PARS. A beginning travel agent would have little trouble deciding which system to learn.

If you're looking for a new job in the same field, the classifieds can tell you which specialties within that occupation are in demand. In the *Times* ads for legal secretaries, a knowledge of litigation was mentioned 17 times. Three specialties—real estate, negligence and estates/trusts—rated six mentions each. Corporate law experience was called for three times. Entertainment, medical malpractice, patent and domestic law were mentioned in one ad each.

If you've had some experience in one of the more popular specialties, you can rewrite your résumé to emphasize it. And if you have no experience in the specialties employers seem to be looking for, you've learned that signing up for a seminar or evening course in real estate law or negligence might be helpful.

Want ads can tell you not only about specific jobs, but about the kinds of employers who are hiring these days. You can learn what to major in (or what you should have majored in), the kind of experience you need for the next step up the corporate ladder and sometimes the personal attributes employers seek in your occupation. A recent Sunday listing of ads for marketing research specialists, for instance, turned up the following information.

Who's hiring: 4 market research firms, 1 package goods corporation, 1 package goods ad agency, 1 importer, 1 supplier, 1 transportation equipment leasing company, 1 health and beauty division of a national corporation.

Average salary: $33,600, with jobs listed from $22,000 to $50,000.

Required education: 3 mentioned marketing majors, 1 an MBA and 1 a graduate degree in experimental psychology.

Where should you have worked in the past? 2 called for agency experience, 2 for supplier experience, 1 for corporate experience, 1 for consumer experience.

What kinds of duties should you have handled? Focus groups (2 mentions), questionnaire design and analysis, interviewing, in-depth interviews, client contact (1 mention each).

What other special skills should you have? Statistics, 5 mentions. Computer knowledge and writing/communication skills, 3 each. Detail-oriented, 2. Analytic skills, data-oriented skills and good marketing perspective, 1 mention each.

If you're still in school and planning a career in marketing research, you've now learned that a marketing major and statistics minor is ideal. If you're relatively new to the field, you've picked up some important buzzwords to use at courtesy interviews. And even if you're an experienced marketing researcher, you've learned something about where you might direct your own inquiries.

The news you learn in the classified ads can be depressing, especially if your field is a competitive one. But this might be a blessing in disguise. In a recent batch of 30 editorial job ads, for instance, 13 asked for math, science, or medical backgrounds and 10 were for computer or electronics publications. There were three jobs each for food industry and financial/business writers. Only four ads were for more traditional specialties—children's books, remedial reading, fashion and retailing.

The out-of-work journalism major, therefore, can improve his job-hunting prospects by signing up for courses in math, science, or data processing, doing volunteer writing or editing for a hospital, or adding sample work in the aforementioned subjects to his portfolio.

When analyzing the classifieds, don't be misled by repeats. Four editorial jobs for metal-producing publications may be ads from four agencies listing the same job—not a sign that metal-producing industry editors are in sudden demand.

Who Else Is Hiring?

After selecting any ads you want to answer, go through the entire classified section from accountant to word processor, looking for ads placed by employers themselves. These can be leads to companies that are expanding.

If Sterling Drug is looking for computer operators this week, they may need financial analysts or purchasing agents next week. If Merrill Lynch is hiring secretaries, they may be expanding in certain departments. Send a cover letter and résumé now, and you could be ahead of the crowd. If a company's name appears several times in the classifieds—advertising for three or more job categories—that's an even better sign.

Some ads will give you an employer profile ("We are a Fortune 250 corporation specializing in pharmaceutical products"), possibly mentioning new areas of growth. The name and address of the personnel contact are often listed, but don't write him. He's busy filling this job, and your résumé could be lost amid the stacks of hundreds that are coming in.

Instead, call the company's main number and ask for the department in which you'd like to work. Ask for the name of the department vice president or another executive who heads that section. If asked for your reasons, reply that you'd like to write a letter to that person. If you're asked "Is this about employment?", say no. Do be sure to ask for the correct spelling of the person's name and his or her exact job title.

Send a letter highlighting your qualifications for a job in that department. Mention the reasons you'd want to work specifically for this company, and make them convincing. Ask for an appointment to talk about possible openings, and follow up with a phone call. You may want to enclose a résumé, or wait to bring one along at the meeting.

Should You Answer Blind Ads?

Yes, say the experts. Blind ads are those that ask you to write to an anonymous box number, but they're much less mysterious than they seem.

"Companies sometimes run blind ads for cost reasons," one

job consultant explains. "They may get 500 responses, and it's just too expensive—in terms of staff time—to send out 499 'thank you, but no thank you' notes." The blind ad gets them off the hook.

Blind ads also may be run because the person who's being replaced has no idea he or she is on the way out. Companies run blind ads occasionally to do a little research. The responses tell them about the job market for this occupation, the kinds of backgrounds they can expect to find among applicants and what they'll be able to get away with paying for a similar job in the future.

What if you suspect the ad has been placed by your own employer? Take the chance and answer it, say headhunters. You can attach a note to your response, saying "If the client for this ad is the XYZ Company, please do not forward my résumé." Many newspapers will honor your requests. An agency handling the search often will protect you in the same way.

Don't forget to read the classified ads in trade journals as well as in your local newspaper. For advice on getting noticed when you answer an ad, see Step 11.

Bowl Them Over With a Cover Letter

Why: A naked résumé is an insult. And a well-written cover letter can make you stand out in ways a résumé alone never can.

Time: 30 minutes or less per letter

One executive search firm that never runs ads for its $50,000-and-up jobs ran one in a trade journal last year. The owner was amazed at one result. More than half the résumés arrived unaccompanied by any kind of cover letter.

"Sometimes a cover letter is only a courtesy, like saying please or thank you, but it's an important one," explains the owner. "When a résumé comes in without one, the person who sent it is saying two things. 'I don't care enough about getting this job to bother writing you directly.' And 'I'm sending my résumé to every ad in the paper, which is why I don't have time to write even a short note.' Both these messages are insulting, and are good ways not to get an interview."

Even if you feel your résumé speaks for itself, be professional enough to accompany it with at least a one-paragraph message, typed neatly and signed by hand.

Dear Sir or Madam:
Enclosed is my résumé in response to your ad for a
Senior Project Leader which appeared in the May 3
edition of the *Atlanta Journal*. I look forward to
hearing from you.

Sincerely,

With a little additional effort, however, a cover letter can
be much more than courteous. It can make a big difference
in getting your résumé noticed, by dramatically pointing out
your qualifications for the job.

Anne Sweeney, who runs a résumé service in addition to
her work for Inter-Continental Hotels, likes the two-column
approach comparing "Your Needs" (as outlined in the ad) and
"My Skills and Experience." The system might work like this.

The Ad

ADMIN ASST./SEC'Y $20–24,000 + !
SHOW BIZ
I'm looking for an ass't for a very well known VIP in
this industry. This unusual oppty is avail for a unique
indiv who has gd commun skls (written & verbal),
sophistication, a prof'l manner & the presence to
handle high level execs, clients & key figures in the
entertainment industry! Coll a definite + —your
years of exp not as critical as your wk exp (corp
bkgrnd)—own corresp (type nec). By appt. only.

The Letter

Dear Sir or Madam:
I'm writing in response to your ad for an entertainment
industry administrative assistant/secretary in the April
10 *New York Times*. This certainly sounds like a
challenging opportunity, and I believe my
qualifications match your client's requirements quite
well.

Good communications skills/written and verbal	Verbal skills rated in 98th percentile on college entrance examinations
	Public speaking experience
Sophistication/ professional manner	Four year's experience in arranging business entertainment
	International travel to six countries
Presence to handle high-level executives, clients and entertainment figures	Daily business contact with CEOs and political dignitaries in most recent job
College	Two years' study at Converse College, including courses in business writing and secretarial science
Corporate work experience	Five years' experience working for Fortune 500 corporations, including three years at headquarters office
Own correspondence/typing	Have handled own correspondence in all jobs to date, averaging 30–50 letters per month in most recent assignment
	Typing speed: 70 words per minute

My résumé is enclosed. I will call your office later this week in the hope of arranging an appointment.

Very truly yours,

Although the hypothetical applicant who wrote this hypothetical letter has no experience in the entertainment industry, she has a much better than average chance of getting an interview for this glamour job. That's because her cover letter has accomplished its objectives.

- It tells the employment agency counselor or personnel department representative that she has *all* the qualifications the hiring manager said he was looking for.
- It makes an effort to quantify some intangible job qualifications like "sophistication" and "presence."
- It proves she's truly interested in the job. Otherwise, why would she have taken the time to write such a detailed letter, tailored to this one position?
- It highlights important aspects of her work experience, which appear on her résumé in another format.
- It discourages the agency or personnel department representative's tendency to throw away the cover letter before passing it on. After all, the letter is his rationale for having selected the résumé to begin with.

In some cases, a shorter cover letter may be appropriate. When an ad mentions few specific qualifications (or none at all), this three-paragraph form makes your points effectively.

The Ad

CHEMIST Fee pd To $50m
Cosmetics, nail lacquer, mfg. exp.

The Letter

Gentlemen/Ladies:
This is in response to your ad for a Chemist in the September 22 *Washington Post*.
My ten years of business experience include six years in the cosmetic industry. As a Senior Research

Scientist with Devereux International, I am responsible for a number of nail lacquer formulations and was part of the research team handling last year's successful $10 million launch of the "Space Age Frosts" collection. I am a contributing editor of *Cosmetic Research Quarterly* and hold a Ph.D. in chemistry from UCLA.

I would welcome the opportunity to discuss my qualifications in greater detail at a personal interview. I look forward to hearing from you.

Sincerely,

Rules for the Cover Letter

1. *Type it,* single-spaced, with a professional machine. If you can't type or have access only to an antique Smith-Corona portable, pay a friend to type your correspondence. Offer anything from minimum wage to $5 per hour, or make a barter arrangement.

2. *Use the right paper.* Business-like personal stationery is ideal, but not necessary. Instead ask your stationery-store clerk for a plain white bond in at least a 20-pound weight. Recruiters are divided about 50-50 on whether you can get away with writing on your current employer's letterhead. Personal stationery bordered with butterflies, tiny football players or three-masted sailing ships is a serious mistake.

3. *Address the recruiter by name* whenever possible. Sometimes the name is listed in the ad. Sometimes, if you call (anonymously), the agency or personnel department will tell you who is handling the search. Otherwise, use "Dear Sir or Madam," "Gentlemen/Ladies," or "To: The John Doe Agency."

4. *Mention where you heard of the job.* If you're answering a classified ad, mention the date and publication in which you saw the ad. If this is a personal recommendation, mention that person by name: "Catherine Carson of your budget analysis department

recommended I get in touch with you in connection with a possible opening in the professional sales division."

5. *Keep it simple.* Be polite and professional, but use straightforward, easy-to-read language as much as possible. All the rules for business correspondence apply to cover letters, only more so.

6. *Don't forget to enclose your résumé.*

12

Work With Agencies

Why: In some fields, it's the most likely way to get hired. In others, it's the only way to switch jobs discreetly.

Time: Half an hour to sign up

When you're 21 and fresh out of school with few professional contacts, signing up with an employment agency is a good way to get a job search started. When you're 51 and a top executive with high industry visibility, working through an executive search firm is the only way to let other companies know you're available.

Personnel agencies may be most valuable at the beginning of your career and at its peak, but they should be part of your job search at every level. Some employers don't want to be bombarded with résumés when they have a plum job opening, and are willing to pay agency fees in order to have those specialists do all the screening.

SEARCH FIRMS AND AGENCIES: WHAT'S IN A NAME?

Despite the various names employment specialists give their organizations, there are really only two kinds of companies: the kind you can phone, and the kind that will phone you. The former is a *personnel agency.* You see the names of these companies in the classified ads and, if you're interested in a particular job they're handling, you can call them or send your résumé. Even if you haven't seen a particular job but you know that they handle hiring in your field, you may be able to make an appointment and meet with one of the agency counselors in order to be considered for any future openings they handle. Personnel agencies handle all kinds of jobs, from clerical to executive. Many do specialize in certain fields, however, and some only handle management jobs.

The second kind of organization, the *executive search firm,* will find you—if you're earning over $40,000 a year or should be. These professionals have become known as headhunters because they will happily steal a Lever Brothers VP to fill a spot at Colgate-Palmolive, or vice versa. That's what they're in business for.

It works something like this. A company has an opening for a new sales vice president, so they call in a search firm to tell them the type of person they'd like to find. The search-firm specialist tries to pin them down as much as possible. "What kind of company do you want this person to come from? Does it have to be one of your direct competitors, or could the person be from a firm in a related industry?"

Then the search-firm people start making phone calls. "We call people at those target companies," explains Linda Kline of Kline-McKay. "We ask people there if they might be interested in this spot. And if not, do they know someone else who would be right for this position? You get to know a lot of people over the years, but we do call total strangers at times. And we go through business and association directories and our own files to find possible candidates."

Working With a Search Firm

Gary Marshall, vice president of Smyth Dawson Associates, a search firm based in Stamford, Connecticut, agrees. "About 80 percent of the people we recommend are already known to us," he estimates. "We may not have talked to a particular candidate in three years, but we'll call and interview him if he's right for a position that comes open."

Marshall meets with the candidate, draws up a Candidate Profile Report and sends that to the client company. The average search takes two to six months.

A search firm is given a retainer by the client company as payment for finding the person to fill the job. Contingency agencies, who often work with lower-paying jobs, are paid only if and when they find the person eventually hired. Therefore, several agencies may have the job listed. But either an agency or a search firm may work on an "exclusive contingency" basis, which means that no other firm can send you on an interview for that job (because no one else is handling it), but the firm is paid only if it succeeds in finding the right candidate. It's perfectly acceptable for you to ask an agency or search firm, "Are you the only one working on this?"

Should you bother sending your résumé to a search firm? It's a long shot, but it can't hurt. It probably will be placed in the files and given a once-over when a job in your field comes up.

The best way to make yourself known to a search firm is to build a strong professional reputation. The second best way is through personal recommendation. Ask friends which headhunters have called them or gotten them jobs in the past. Then a friend may call that firm on your behalf, or allow you to use his name when you call or write.

Don't worry if you've never heard of the search firm that calls you. Most do no advertising at all. At the most, they may run an occasional trade journal ad or look for candidates via direct mail campaigns.

Choosing an Agency

The ideal way to choose an agency is the same way they like to choose you—through someone you both know. Ask friends which agencies they've worked with and been happy with. Then check out the newspaper classifieds, looking for agencies that specialize in jobs like the one you're looking for. Just be sure to stay away from

- Agencies that charge you the fee, instead of having it paid by the employer.
- Agencies that ask you to sign a contract for career counseling. (The only thing you should sign is an agreement not to leave any job they find for you within a certain time period.)
- Agencies that strike you as sleazy when you visit their offices. (Luxurious offices, however, are no guarantee of company integrity. Try to judge the people, rather than the decor.)
- Agencies that assure you the job you saw advertised is still available but, when you arrive to sign up, tell you it's just been filled.

WILL AN AGENCY BE ABLE TO PLACE YOU?

If you're trying to switch fields or make any kind of out-of-the-ordinary job change, probably not. Whether you work with a search firm or a personnel agency, the person you're working with is being paid by the client company and has their interests at heart.

"The only time I ever persuaded a client to see someone with experience that didn't exactly fit was when the job candidate was an old friend of mine," admits an agency employee. "And even then he didn't get the job. If we want to keep that company's business, we're going to send them what they ask for—not people we happen to want to help." Career switchers are better off using personal contacts and answering employer-placed ads to get interviews.

People in certain career fields are more likely to be placed by agencies. "We ran an ad for Communications Writers and got 850 résumés," notes a financial services company recruiter. "Why should we pay a $12,000 agency fee when we can get results like that? Yet we hire 90 percent of our computer programmers through agencies."

Other specialists usually hired through agencies include accountants from Big 8 firms, telecommunications engineers and any specialists with technical skills. The less competitive your field, the more likely you are to be placed by an agency.

WHAT WILL AN AGENCY DO FOR YOU?

It depends on the agency and on the motivation of the counselor you work with. At the least you can expect them to pass along your résumé and set up the interview. Because it's in their interest to make a placement, they may give you insight into the people you'll be meeting with at the client company and what they seem to be looking for.

The agency will make follow-up calls to find out what's going on. They'll even negotiate salary, if there's a question about it. When it's bad news, they'll let you know that you've been counted out. Many times they'll be able to tell you why, honestly, so that you can work on the problem, if there is one. The agency will tell you if the selection has been narrowed down to you and one or two others, but they usually can't or won't tell you the names of the other finalists.

SHOULD YOU BE HONEST WITH AGENCIES?

Never lie about your experience, education or any of the tangibles on your résumé and application. If you're found out, both you and the agency will lose credibility with the client company—leaving you with two business enemies.

If you have doubts about whether a particular job is right for you, keep it to yourself. The agency person wants to make a placement and might try to sell you on the company involved. On the other hand, he or she might begin pushing another job candidate if he or she senses your indecision. Talk over the problem with friends and family instead.

13

Coordinate Your Interview Wardrobe

Why: The book *Dress for Success* brought it to everyone's attention. We're judged by what we wear, and first impressions count.

Time: 20 minutes looking over your closet, or one afternoon shopping

Imagine that you're interviewing three qualified people for a job. One woman appears in a scoop-neck knit dress. The man arrives in a crumpled suit with a stain on his tie. And the third applicant, a woman, is dressed neatly in a color-coordinated jacket, blouse and skirt. Which candidate has the edge?

If you can't appear businesslike and pulled-together for an interview, recruiters assume you won't be able to do it for work every day. "Everyone I've ever hired dressed better for their interview than they ever did again," reports a Young & Rubicam advertising executive. "But that's understandable. They were putting their best foot forward."

THE BUSINESSWOMAN'S GUIDE TO INTERVIEW DRESSING

No one ever lost out on a job by dressing too conservatively or looking too businesslike.

- Play it safe and wear neutral colors: beige, brown, gray or black. Pastels aren't professional.
- Wear a skirt, never pants.
- Save super-feminine items like lace blouses or pink angora sweaters for evening wear. The idea is to look professional, not seductive.
- Leave gaudy or dangling jewelry at home. It's too distracting.
- Don't wear or carry anything covered with designer initials.
- A little hat and white gloves were the rule in 1950s offices. Times have changed.
- Don't wear anything frivolous. Sweaters with knitted-in street scenes may be expensive, but they make a clear statement: "Don't take me seriously."
- Don't outdress the interviewer. Leave obviously expensive clothes in your closet until you've gotten the job.
- Dress as though you already represent the company.
- Go beyond neat; be immaculate.
- Have your shoes reheeled and shined.
- Suits are nice, but a blouse, skirt and vest can look just as businesslike.
- Use color-coordinated scarves and accessories to add polish to your outfit.

Things would be simpler if you had only one interview to worry about. But even candidates for clerical jobs are often called back more than once. Four or five interviews at one company is no longer considered out of the ordinary, so you'll need at least three businesslike ensembles coordinated and ready to wear.

SAVING MONEY ON INTERVIEW CLOTHES

If you already have an attractive wardrobe of business clothes, coming up with three outfits is no problem. But if you're unemployed, the cost of new clothes is probably not in your budget. If you're a new graduate, you'll probably have to start a business wardrobe from scratch. And no matter what your financial status, you've probably complained about the escalating prices of women's fashions. To build an interview wardrobe without having to take out a loan, consider these ideas:

- Forget suits; they're too expensive. Build your wardrobe from separates: unstructured jackets and inexpensive vests worn over blouses and skirts. You get more variety for the money.
- Be sure all three interview outfits can be worn with the same color accessories. That way you'll only need brown shoes and bag or black shoes and bag, not both.
- Shop for designer fashions in discount stores.
- Learn how to sew.
- If you're all thumbs, pay a friend to sew for you. Or offer your typing, writing, designing or other professional services in exchange.
- For the most variety at the lowest cost, follow the wardrobe advice to men in the next section. Just substitute scarves for ties, and vests for suit jackets.

THE EXECUTIVE LOOK FOR MEN

Mortimer Levitt, founder and owner of the Custom Shop shirtmakers chain, recommends a few simple rules to make any man look like the executive he is, or should be. To build an impeccable interview wardrobe, follow this advice:

- *Always wear one fancy and two plains.* That means a solid shirt, solid tie and patterned suit, or a solid suit, solid shirt and patterned tie, or a solid suit, solid tie and patterned shirt. The look is low-key, Levitt explains, and projects "an image of substance."
- *Always wear a base color (your suit) with an accent color (your shirt and/or tie).* Examples: gray suit with blue shirt with gray and blue tie; navy suit with yellow shirt with navy and yellow tie. A third color in the tie is fine, as long as the accent and base are included.
- *Always wear light with dark, and dark with light.* In most cases, your suit will be dark and your shirt light. But light suits call for darkish shirts. The contrast gives your look character.
- *Wear a shirt collar that fits perfectly—especially at front and back.* "The one article of clothing that will change your appearance more radically than anything else you wear," says Levitt, "is a shirt collar fitted to four dimensions, instead of the usual two." Buying shirts in quarter sizes (15¼ or 15¾, instead of 15½, for instance) is the first step. But men should also be sure that the collar back is high enough for the length of their necks. Collar-front height depends on your age and the angle at which your neck is positioned to your body. Custom-made shirts solve the problem.

Other ways to make a good interview impression:

- The plain gray flannel suit: The first business attire you should buy.
- The Ivy League suit.
- A solid-color knit tie.
- End-on-end broadcloth shirts: Very elegant.
- A good attache case: Imperative.
- The classic 3½-inch tie width, no matter what the extremes of fashion dictate.
- Silk ties, if you can afford them; polyester, if you can't.
- Monogrammed linen handkerchiefs.

Absolute Don'ts

- Cashmere or silk suits, which hold their shapes poorly.
- Home-laundered and home-pressed shirts.

For more information: *The Executive Look/How to Get It—How to Keep It*
By Mortimer Levitt (Atheneum, 1981).

14

Give Yourself a Good-Looks Makeover

Why: **An attractive male or female face can open doors.**

Time: **Half an hour to three weeks, depending on what you decide to do**

Looks matter, although many will deny it. "Because of new laws and the possibility of being accused of discrimination, nobody hiring or interviewing you is going to say a word about your appearance," admits an insurance company personnel interviewer. "That message really gets stressed at the equal employment seminars we go to. So you're not going to hear constructive criticism from the interviewer, unless he's stupid or willing to risk his job."

The same interviewer confirms that she's always influenced by looks. "In that split second when the job candidate enters the office, you really get the picture. This immediate first impression is the most important moment of the interview. It's never forgotten, and it usually can't be reversed."

Being beautiful or handsome is part of the picture. Studies show that teachers from kindergarten to university can look at exactly the same schoolwork, but will give it a higher grade if they believe it's been done by an attractive person. In adult life that goes for a résumé or a marketing report too.

And looking business-appropriate and well-groomed is equally important. A man who takes the trouble to dress for success in gray flannel ruins the image if his hair is not styled well. A woman can dress for an interview in a tailored suit and carry an expensive attaché, but no employer is going to take her seriously if she's wearing iridescent plum eye shadow, heavy lip gloss and three-inch-long nails. It's your responsibility to look as attractive as possible while fitting into the corporate mold. This can be more complicated for women.

Hair Styles for Women

Studies show that for women in business the best hair styles are neat and simple, anywhere from ear-length to just below the chin, and never longer than shoulder-length. Keep these office hair style taboos in mind.

Ponytails	Too young and casual for an office. If you must pull your hair back, put the band at the nape of your neck.
Frizzy perms	Still considered too trendy or nonconformist, even though the look first made the hair style magazines in the early '70s. If you already have a perm, tame it with electric rollers for your weekday look.
Hair pulled straight back in chignon	Too prim and severe, unless you have the sculptured cheekbones of Jaclyn Smith.
Braids	Looks too trendy or too casual.
Bouffant	Extremely outdated.
Hair ornaments	Anything more noticeable than a tortoise-shell comb or clip is too frivolous for the office.

Hair Coloring for Women

Just about any hair color is fine for businesswomen, as long as it looks natural. The only don'ts are exaggerated colors such as platinum blonde, blue-black, red-orange and the rainbow of punk pastels.

Most people think men with a little gray at the temples look distinguished. Yet women with the same amount of gray are perceived as looking a bit unpolished or "too old." Gray hair does tend to drain color from the face, so that you lose something of your look of vitality—no matter how healthy you are.

Hair coloring is universally accepted, so don't be afraid to cover the gray for a younger, more dynamic look. A permanent shampoo-in color lasts until it grows out and needs retouching every month or so. Semi-permanent products like Loving Care or Color Renewal System last through several shampoos and are extra-gentle because they contain no peroxide. Choose a shade that matches your own natural overall color.

John Molloy vetoed frosting, tipping and streaking in *The Woman's Dress for Success Book,* noting that it tested as "unsexy, lower class and unauthoritative." But he didn't include (or didn't know about) the subtle coloring process called highlighting. It differs from the other methods in that color is applied to very thin, delicate strands of hair (not big chunks) and is usually just a shade or two lighter than your overall color, providing a more natural-looking contrast. It's an ideal way to cover gray, and can make hair look healthier; it usually requires only three or four applications a year.

Makeup for the Interview

Wearing too much makeup is a serious mistake, but eliminating makeup entirely isn't the answer.

"If a woman walked into a job interview with no makeup at all," observes a corporate manager, "I'd assume she was a *hausfrau,* a religious fanatic or someone who just didn't care enough to bother." Luckily, the middle ground on makeup is easy to find.

- Tone down your normal makeup colors for the job interview. That means neutral eyeshadows (browns and grays, not blues and greens), peachy lipsticks (not bright reds) and plain black mascara.
- Forget lip gloss.
- Wear only a dab of blusher. Streaks or circles of cheek color are the mistake mentioned most often by beauty experts and personnel interviewers.
- Check your makeup under fluorescent lights (the way you'll be seen in most offices) or in a lighted makeup mirror on the office-light setting.
- Most important: Wear a foundation that matches your skin tone. When shopping for it, test it on your neck, not your hand, for a perfect match.
- Get a professional manicure, or give yourself one at home. Chewed nails or ragged cuticles make you look like the nervous type.
- Nails should not be longer than half an inch or so.
- Clear, red, coral or muted nail polish shades are fine, but chipped polish makes a terrible impression. If you can't keep nails perfect, wear clear polish instead.

Skin Care for Women and Men

Whether you're 18, 68 or somewhere in between, complexion problems can occur and make a big difference in your looks. No matter what the commercials say, washing your face with bath soap is not a good skin-care ritual—especially if your skin has large pores, is flaky or has a tendency to create blemishes.

"People still get acne in their 30s and 40s," Lydia Sarfati, owner of New York's Klisar Skin Care Center, reminds us. "The one simple step they can take to remedy it is to have their skin professionally cleaned on a regular basis." That means having blackheads squeezed and whiteheads removed in a clean professional atmosphere—not by some mysterious machine, but by the two trained hands of a skin-care expert or dermatologist.

Both men and women can have younger-looking skin by keeping it hydrated. Dehydrated skin lacks water while dry skin has too little oil, but many people confuse the two. Hydrate from the inside out by drinking six to eight glasses of water or fruit juice per day. Hydrate on the outside by using a humidifier at home and by following a twice-a-day routine of cleansing (with a creamy cleanser designed for your skin type), toning (with a mild astringent), and moisturizing.

When skin is hydrated, wrinkles and tiny lines become less visible. Mild acne scars become less apparent too, because the skin around them is "puffed up" with moisture. If you have deep or truly disfiguring scars, however, you may want to see a cosmetic surgeon about dermabrasion or chemical peeling to remove them.

Plastic Surgery

It's against the law for an employer to consider you too old to do a job, but age discrimination takes place every day. If you haven't climbed as far up the corporate ladder as you feel you should have at your age, or if you're returning to the work force—probably to be surrounded by much younger people—there's no reason to look older than necessary. Both men and women have eye tucks and complete facelifts every day.

If you decide on cosmetic surgery, find a board-certified plastic surgeon (the local medical society, friends who've undergone facelifts and your own family physician can help you), talk and think about the decision, then schedule a period of absence. Doctors estimate you'll need three weaks to heal, so you may want to announce a long vacation. Then you can explain your youthful new look by saying you've lost weight, have been to a health spa, have gotten a well-deserved rest or a little of all three.

Are you ready for a facelift? One New York surgeon has a few patients in their twenties, but 45–55 is the average age. You can expect the results to last five to ten years.

Men's Hair Styles and Color

A good hair cut by a stylist is an important part of your image. Any short, neat style is acceptable.

Although society considers a gray-haired man distinguished, you may not agree. If you feel your graying hair is unflattering or simply makes you look older than your years, color it. All the products made for women work equally well on men's hair.

Hair Care for Women and Men

Keeping hair clean and neat is the most important factor for both sexes. Be sure dead ends or damaged hair has been trimmed off. Shampoo and condition hair within 24 hours before a job interview. Use an anti-dandruff shampoo if you have even a hint of flaking. And if you've been out in the wind, take time to comb your hair in the office washroom before making your interview entrance.

15

Give Yourself Speech Lessons

Why: To polish your grammar, accent and speaking style. Sometimes what you say may be ignored because of how you say it.

Time: 30 minutes to several months, depending on your needs

M.J. came to New York, fresh from Atlanta with her brand-new MBA. She was attractive, well-dressed and, by all accounts, brilliant. The problem arose when she opened her mouth. M.J.'s interviewing skills were sharp, and she had all the right answers, but they were spoken with the grammar, dialect and accent of the Deep South. Finally, a headhunter leveled with her ("No one else is going to tell you what the problem is") and recommended that she take diction lessons. Only then did her career get underway.

The world is full of regional and cultural biases, and they work both ways: people are impressed when they call an office and a secretary answers with a British accent, but have the opposite reaction to diction that clearly comes from the Bronx. And that's why Henry Higgins could dress up Eliza Doolittle in a diamond tiara and Paris gown, but couldn't take her anywhere until he taught her how to speak.

Your voice may not speak well of you, but there are ways to eliminate any problem.

Pinpointing Your Problem

If you have a serious speech defect, like stuttering, you should seek help from a speech pathologist or other professional. But if your problem is a regional accent, a speaking style that people associate with low socio-economic status or a simple lack of grammatical knowledge, even your best friends may never tell you.

- Ask a friend who's confident of her or his verbal skills if you mispronounce or misuse any words. Ask for specific examples.
- Tape-record your voice in normal conversation with a friend. Let the tape run for at least 15–20 minutes, so you can forget about it and fall into your usual speech patterns. Play it back and listen for any problems or bad habits.
- If you've moved from the country to the city, or from one section of the U.S. to another, what do people say about your regional accent? "What a charming accent" may be a polite reaction masking a more negative opinion.
- When you finally meet people you've often talked to over the phone, do they express surprise at how differently they imagined you? Do they find you more attractive, younger, older, more sophisticated? You may need to improve your voice.

Getting Help

The easiest and most effective way to improve your speaking voice is to take lessons. If you aren't familiar with a good teacher, look in the Yellow Pages under speech improvement, voice or diction. Then check out the school or teacher you choose by asking for the names of former clients and calling them to ask if they were satisfied with the results. Judge for yourself when you hear their voices.

Formal classes aren't the only answer. If you live in a small city where such instruction isn't available, or if you feel you don't need that much help, there are other means of self-improvement.

- Buy English-language records or tapes at a large bookstore. They were developed for foreign visitors or residents learning English as a second language, but can help you perfect your pronunciation too.
- Buy a book that lists the words most often mispronounced in English. Check those you use in daily conversation and words you might use in an interview.
- If grammar is one of your problems, sign up for a night course in remedial English. Don't put it on your résumé.
- Take a few lessons at home with a private tutor. An English teacher or college English major can help you with grammar and vocabulary. A local disc jockey or TV reporter probably has had training in nonregional speech.

CORRECT YOUR GRAMMAR IN ONE EASY LESSON

"As I was getting off of the plane," said the applicant, "I axed myself—what is the single most important criteria for this job? Mr. Jones told my wife and I that this opportunity is very unique."

Everybody makes mistakes once in a while, but if you don't spot five obvious errors in the quote above, a quick lesson is in order. Some of the most common English errors are on the following list. Correct even one or two of them in your speech, and you've improved the impression you'll leave behind at the interview.

1. A/AN. Use "a" before words beginning with a consonant, "an" before words beginning with a vowel. "A good speaking voice is *an* asset."

2. AIN'T. There is no correct use of this word in the English language, except in humor or slang. You don't want to use either at a job interview.

3. AMONG/BETWEEN. If you're talking about more than two items, use among. "Just *between* the two of us, few people are able to choose *among* several job offers."

4. ATHLETE. Pronounced with two syllables, not ath-uh-lete.

5. BAD/BADLY and GOOD/WELL. You may feel bad about the news you just heard. If you feel badly, that means something is wrong with your sense of touch. Red looks good on you. If red looked well on you, it would mean that the red had eyes and extremely good vision. Many intelligent and educated people still make this mistake; it's not the worst one you could make.

6. CAN/MAY. Asking permission, you always use "may." "*May* I call you next week?" The word "can" refers to the ability to do something. "I *can* look into that."

7. CONGRATULATIONS. Pronounced con-grach-u-lay-shuns. Not con-grad-u-lay-shuns.

8. CRITERION is a singular. "One important *criterion* is job experience, but there are several *criteria* involved." The same goes for one phenomenon, two phenomena.

9. GRADUATED. You graduated from high school or college. People do say "graduated high school," but it's not quite correct.

10. HEIGHT. Pronounced hite, not heighth.

11. HIMSELF is the correct word, never hisself. Themselves, never theirselves.

12. HOPEFULLY is frequently used, but still incorrect. Instead of "Hopefully I'll hear from you soon," say "I'll hope to hear from you soon."

13. IF I WERE. Use the subjunctive correctly. "If I were" and "If he or she were" are usually correct, not "If I was."

14. INFER/IMPLY. This is another error commonly made by otherwise knowledgeable people. To imply is to hint at something without saying it outright. To infer is to observe something and come to a conclusion. If you suggest that your boss take remedial English, you're implying that he doesn't speak correctly. If your boss sees a new résumé on your desk, he may infer that you're looking for a new job.

15. IRREGARDLESS is not a word. Say regardless, if you're going to say anything at all.

16. IRREPARABLE is pronounced ir-rep'-er-able, not ir-re-pair'-a-ble.

17. LAW is not pronounced lor. Saw is not pronounced sor.

18. LAY/LIE. One of the most complicated conjugations in English. In general, living things lie and inanimate objects lay, but the conjugations overlap and meanings differ. "I *lie* down at night, I *lay* down last night, I have *lain* in wait for hours. I will *lay* the pencil on the table. I *laid* it there yesterday." If you're unsure of the right form to use, avoid using it at all.

19. LESS/FEWER. Use less if the noun in question is measured, fewer if it can be counted. "This job takes *less* sales experience than some others and will require *fewer* days on the road." All the commercials that talk about "less calories" are wrong. They mean "fewer calories."

20. LIKE/AS IF. A noun or gerund is preceded by "like"; a clause is preceded by "as if" or "as though." So "he looks *like* an executive, and she looks *as if* she's an executive already."

21. LIKE TO HAVE. "I like to have missed this appointment" is substandard English. "I almost missed this appointment" is correct.

22. MEDIA is the plural of medium. Many people say "the news media is responsible for this," but that's incorrect. "The news media—newspapers, TV, radio—are responsible."

23. UNIQUE. This word means one of a kind and cannot be modified. If you say "very unique," you're saying "very one of a kind." Either it's unique or it's not.
24. OFF OF is never correct. Just say off.
25. REAL/REALLY. In current slang, educated people say "I was real nervous about that presentation." In an interview, say really.
26. RELEVANT. Pronounced re-le-vant, not rev-e-lant.
27. SHOULD/COULD/WOULD OF. You probably mean should have, could have or would have.
28. CONNOTATION. When using the verb form, say "connote," not "connotate." The same goes for orientation. You want to orient yourself to a new situation, not orientate.
29. VEHICLE. Pronounced with an accent on the first syllable, never the second.
30. WHO/WHOM. Who is a subject; whom is an object. Always say "with whom" and "for whom."
31. WE/US and I/ME. "I and we" are subjects; "me and us" are objects. "The report will be forwarded to Bill and me" is correct, not "Bill and I." Would you say "The report will be forwarded to I?"
32. DOUBLE NEGATIVES are always wrong. Words like hardly and scarcely are considered negatives. Say "I can hardly believe the news," not "I can't hardly believe."

4 EASY RULES FOR MAKING A GOOD VERBAL IMPRESSION

1. *Stay away from slang.* Your last job was not a bummer; it was an unfortunate experience.
2. *Keep it clean.* Never use four-letter words during an interview. Say "darn" and "heck," even if you think you sound like the *Andy Griffith Show*.

3. *Avoid technical jargon,* unless the interviewer has used the term first.
4. *Stay away from terms and pronunciations you're unsure of.* This is not the time to practice using a newly learned word. Keep it simple, and you'll communicate effectively.

Rehearse the Interview

Why: **The interview will make you or break you, and most of us need practice in speaking highly of ourselves.**

Time: **15–20 minutes**

"All the things people ask on interviews and all the variations really boil down to about ten basic questions," believes one personnel department VP. That's why going into your first interview without having given some thought to your answers is a needless—and serious—mistake.

Take a look at these frequently asked questions and think over your answers. You may even want to write down the replies you decide are best.

1. *Tell me a little about yourself.* Briefly describe your job history, current position, and professional interests. Don't get any more personal than mentioning the state or country in which you were born and/or the name of the college you attended.
2. *Why are you interested in this particular job?* Perhaps it's a wonderful opportunity to combine your interests and experiences in two fields. Perhaps it's been your long-term goal to work for this company and this department because of its reputation for excellence, innovation or management style. Whatever your answer, make it as sincere and convincing as possible.

3. *What makes you feel you could do this job well?* Discuss specific work experience, education, or skills that can be put to use in this job.
4. *Why do you want to leave your current job?* Make this a positive answer, not a belittling of your current duties, company or supervisor. Perhaps you feel ready to take on new managerial responsibilities and there's nowhere to move up in your current situation. Perhaps you want to take the sales experience you've gotten at the travel agency and put it to work in a corporate environment where you can specialize in the field you've come to enjoy most—incentive travel.
5. *Why did you leave your last job?* Be prepared to answer this question for each of your past jobs. The reasons should always be professional ones, not superficial complaints. Again, be sure to phrase things positively. "I wanted an opportunity to do more writing and work in a creative atmosphere" may describe the same situation as "I was bored just doing administrative work, and the company was very stuffy and old-fashioned." The person who made the former statement is more likely to get hired.
6. *Where do you see yourself in ten years?* "Lying on a beach in Jamaica" is obviously the wrong answer, but so is a reply that sounds too ambitious. This may be a good time to hedge: "That depends on the opportunities that arise during the next few years, but I do know that I'll want to be very much involved with labor relations and working in a corporate setting."
7. *Exactly what do you do at the XYZ Company now?* Describe your duties and responsibilities in specific detail. As much as possible, relate your current duties to those of the job you're interviewing for. This is a good chance to work in the three points about yourself that you listed back in Step 4.
8. *What have you accomplished on this job?* What are you proudest of? In other words, why are you worth the salary they're paying you? Pick one or two accomplishments that relate to the job you're inter-

viewing for, and describe how you used your talents
and experience to get them done.

9. *What would you say is your greatest weakness?* You
can handle this in one of two ways. Either choose a
real weakness that doesn't relate at all to the job
you're interviewing for; or choose a weakness that
could also be construed as a strength (perfectionism,
attention to detail), and balance your answer by
mentioning how it's been an advantage at times.

10. *What do you like most about your current job?* Mention something you'd continue to do, or do even more
of, on this job. And if you're asked what you like least,
make it something that wouldn't arise at this company.

11. *What's the biggest problem you've encountered on
this job?* Don't talk about one that you're still working
on, or one that couldn't be solved. Explain a real
problem, the steps you took to overcome it and the
results.

12. *What areas of your job haven't you been able to handle without supervision or guidance?* Make it clear
that such situations are very rare. You might want to
point out a certain area in which you've asked for
guidance—but only because it was your supervisor's
special area of expertise. In fact, having worked with
him or her now makes you something of an expert in
that area.

13. *How do you plan to reach your long-term goal?* Make
it clear that you do have a plan. Mention special education, training or experience you plan to get in the
next few years. This is a chance to clarify how the
job you're interviewing for is ideal for you and fits
into your plans. You want to demonstrate that you
have the maturity to plan ahead, but never threaten
the interviewer by implying that you're after his or
her job.

14. *How have your original career goals changed since
you got out of school?* Here's your chance to prove
that you're a mature, thoughtful businessperson. This
is another opportunity to work in at least one of your

three major points. Perhaps through your first years in business, you discovered new talents and interests. Point them out, explaining how you've learned to put them to good use in the working world.

15. *What kind of management style would you say you have? What style does your supervisor use?* If you've never attended the managerial grid to learn about "9,9" styles (maximum attention to people and productivity) or read books about Japanese management theory, don't worry. This is a question you should answer vaguely, anyway. To claim one style is to discredit the others, possibly including the interviewer's favorite. Talk about flexibility, different styles for different situations, matching your style to the corporate culture and the people involved.

16. *Do you prefer to work on your own, or as part of a team?* Unless you're applying for a job as sole researcher at the North Pole, your answer must prove that you're a team player. Having worked on corporate committees and task forces would make good credentials in this case.

17. *The job calls for experience in X. Have you done that before?* If you've never sold country music albums to Russian cabinetmakers or whatever this job calls for, be prepared to talk about related experience. You might say something like, "I haven't had that particular experience, but I've given a great deal of thought to the skills needed to do a good job at it. And I feel that the work I did with _____and with _____ were quite similar. That experience, combined with some intense research, getting to know everything there is to know about the Russian cabinetmakers' market, should be good preparation for this job."

Rehearsal Time

Now that you've given some thought to these questions, ask a friend or relative to rehearse the interview with you, playing the role of the hiring manager. Anyone over age 14 will do, but someone with business experience who has been through this before will probably create a more authentic experience.

Give your résumé and the preceding list of 17questions to your friend. Set a kitchen timer for 15 or 20 minutes, sit down and let your friend begin questioning you. If you get the giggles, keep going. If you suddenly feel your answers are all wrong, don't allow yourself the luxury of stopping and asking to start over. Instead practice getting out of it and recovering your credibility—as if this were for real.

Pretend you're on TV. This is not to make you nervous, but to remind you that you're in the spotlight during a job interview. Whenever you're tempted to admit something negative or relax into casual intimacy, just ask yourself, "Would I do or say this on *Eyewitness News?*"

Go through the interview rehearsal as many times as you like, and with as many different friends. You'll feel much more comfortable during a real interview if the situation and questions are familiar. Evaluate yourself by asking if you got across the major selling points about yourself, and whether you said or revealed anything negative about yourself during the interview.

If you're having trouble coming up with the right answers, it could be a mental block about saying good things about your abilities and accomplishments. Be objective and think of yourself as a product which it is your job to sell during this meeting.

"Self-marketing is not a dirty word," career counselor James Malone reminds us. "It's what job hunting is all about."

If you want to rehearse the interview again without a little help from your friends, just write out the questions on separate pieces of paper. You may want to add a few of your own that apply to your situation ("Why have you changed jobs ten times in the past ten years?", "Why do you want to switch from sales promotion to administration?", "Why do you want to take a job after running your own business?").

Put these pieces of paper in a bowl or basket. Set your timer for 15 or 20 minutes, then start pulling questions from the bowl and answering the ones that you draw. For an evaluation, tape the self-interview on a cassette recorder and play it back immediately.

Apply for a Job You Don't Want

Why: Just for practice.

Time: A lunch hour, or an hour after work

You've explained to the man at the personnel agency that you're interested only in working for a large consumer products manufacturer or a firm handling major consumer products accounts. "I have just the thing for you," he announces cheerily. "A great spot at an insurance company downtown. They're looking for someone with experience almost exactly like yours."

Maybe so, but you're not looking for *them*. You worked for an insurance company one summer in high school and hated everything about it. Your first husband was in life insurance, and you've developed an allergy to actuarial tables. Hasn't this man listened to anything you've told him?

Go to the interview. You have nothing to lose, and a lot of important experience to gain.

Play to win, however. Prepare for the interview as if it were the most important one in your life. Keep your energy level up throughout the process, and convince this manager that nothing would make you happier than a career in insurance.

If you can pull off this deception, future declarations of career interest will feel a lot more natural.*

Anyway, new job hunters can use the practice. "Interviewing doesn't come back to you like riding a bicycle," agrees an executive who switched jobs after a decade with the same company. "It's like dating again after 20 years of marriage. Not only does the whole thing feel unfamiliar, but they've changed half the rules since the last time you tried it."

You can learn a number of things from interviewing for a job in which you have no interest:

- Your strengths as an interview subject
- Your weaknesses as an interview subject
- The specific questions a real interviewer asks after having looked at your application and résumé
- The questions you don't handle well
- The subjects that make you nervous
- The value of your most recent work experience and/or education on today's job market, or at least something of how it's regarded
- Any bad habits that emerge during an interview (like nail biting, nervous laughter, etc.)

What to Do About It

Play back the experience in your mind, from the moment you entered the building until you shook hands goodbye. Get out a pen and paper and make two lists: five things you did well and five you could improve on. The first list is just as important as the second, because confidence is an indispensable job-hunting tool. When you walk into the next interview,

---

*Ethical note: If you're invited back for a second interview, don't waste the employer's time by accepting if you're not really interested. These people have a real job to fill, and other things to do.

you'll know ahead of time that you're going to score certain points—and your attitude will reflect that knowledge.

Did you have trouble working in those three important points about yourself? If not, relax and go to the head of the class—as long as bringing them up felt natural and you didn't sense negative reactions from the interviewer.

If you did have trouble finding the right time or method to make your points, take a lesson from TV. Watch how celebrities on talk shows work in the names of their latest books or movies, the names of the people who wrote the screenplays or designed the gowns or the names of the products for which they've recently done commercials. Even among show business veterans, some do it much more gracefully than others. But you can learn from watching bad examples as well as good ones. You also can learn something about clever interviewing techniques by watching TV.

The best way to anticipate the tough questions *you're* bound to be asked is through experience. If you have time and can arrange them, accept three or four interviews for jobs you don't want, all with different employers, of course. Review each one and you'll be more than ready for the real thing.

Apply for a Job You Do Want

Why: Great jobs don't always come knocking at your door. You have to answer an ad, say yes to a headhunter or follow a lead. Then you have to get past Personnel.

Time: 5 minutes and up

Your résumé is perfect. Your interview style is flawless. You dress like the Duke or Duchess of Windsor and speak like William F. Buckley. You've built a reputation within your career field and written cover letters good enough for publication. And what does it get you? A 15-minute meeting with a personnel department interviewer who wouldn't know good work in your specialty from a hole in the ground.

Repress your hostility. The personnel department, believe it or not, serves a purpose—and it's important to make a good impression here if you want the chance to impress the people who actually hire. Think of it as a quiz show in which you have to give the right answers to preliminary questions in order to win a chance at the big prize.

ARE YOU GETTING THE BRUSH-OFF?

But you sent your cover letter and résumé directly to the vice-president of marketing for professional products. Or your uncle—who's a personal friend of the director of operations analysis—set this interview up for you. Have you been sent to Personnel as a polite way of getting you out of their hair? It's possible, but it's just as likely that your real contact at the company is only following accepted company procedure.

"It depends on the company," explains one headhunter. "At some places, Personnel only screens for lower- to middle-level jobs, and you'll be able to bypass them. But at other companies, Personnel is strong. You'll have to see them even if you're being hired as president."

If you answered a classified ad, your résumé may have been picked from the stack by the hiring manager herself. But she has to play by the rules, give her choices to the personnel department interviewer, ask him to screen you and—whether she means it or not—ask for that person's opinion on the candidates seen.

If you were recommended by an agency or search firm, it could work the same way. Whatever the case, your job now is to convince the personnel interviewer that he or she should send you on to the next plateau.

But if they know nothing about your specialty, what are they looking for?

- *People who fit into the corporate culture.* Companies have images and personalities just as individuals do, and one of Personnel's functions is to screen out people who wouldn't fit in. Many a college fraternity man has turned down a freshman rushee for only one reason: "He's just not Sigma Chi (or SAE or Deke) material." Corporations often work the same way. If you don't fit into the culture, you probably wouldn't be happy at the job anyway.
- *People who have the qualifications the hiring manager asked for.* It's even more important to prove this to the personnel interviewer than to the person who will hire you. You can tell the hiring manager, "No, I've never done that, but I have similar experience in _____."

But the personnel recruiter doesn't know your field well enough to judge whether that's really comparable experience. He doesn't want to be criticized by the hiring manager for sending in someone unqualified, so he's likely to count you out.

How do you get around this problem? By careful phrasing you can say yes without lying. Let's say the job description calls for someone with experience in signing up celebrities to speak at university seminars. You've signed up lots of people to speak at seminars, but never anyone famous. On the other hand, you once worked as an administrative assistant at an entertainment management firm and have dealt with dozens of celebrities in a variety of other business situations.

When the interviewer asks "Have you signed up celebrities for seminars?", you can nod and reply, "Yes, I've worked with a number of celebrities over the past seven years." Then name a few. You've been technically honest for now. You can be more precise when you speak to the person who would be your supervisor in the new job.

- *People who really want the job.* Personnel will screen you out immediately if they feel you aren't sure of what you really want to do, that you'd take any job the company offered you in any department or that you might take the job reluctantly and leave after three months. Refer back to Step 1 for tactics you might encounter and possible replies.

SCHEDULING AND RESCHEDULING

What if the company gave you an appointment and then canceled, claiming illness or emergency? Or what if the personnel interviewer assured you that you'd be called back to meet the hiring manager, but you never heard from them?

It's perfectly acceptable to call—or get in touch through your agency—to reschedule.

Yes, they may have changed their minds. But they also may have lost your résumé. Or the person who liked you so much may have been transferred to Chicago. Swallow your pride and find out. The real interview is riding on it.

Research Your Future Employer

Why: Nothing is more insulting than getting all the way to the interview, only to ask "So what do you people make here anyway?"

Time: As little as 10 minutes at the library

"It would be exciting for me to work here," said the secretarial candidate to the ad department executive. "I think your commercials are so creative, especially the 'Reach out and touch someone' campaign."

The candidate can consider that job lost. She's just told an ITT manager how much she loves AT&T's ads. Most job hunters don't make such obvious mistakes, but you can lose points by knowing nothing about the company you're interviewing with. And you can gain a great deal by knowing even a little. Researching a company is also a helpful way to decide whether or not you want to work here.

START AT THE LIBRARY

Many public libraries have opened job information centers where you'll find a number of the references listed here.

Who Are They?

If you're unfamiliar with the company at which you'll be interviewing, your first task is to find out who they are. The *Dun & Bradstreet Million Dollar Directory* lists companies alphabetically, geographically, and by industry. You'll find the company's annual sales, number of employees, divisions, and officers. *Standard & Poor's Register of Corporations* offers similar information. If you're interviewing with a professional association or other nonprofit group, you may find them in the *Encyclopedia of Associations* or *The Foundation Directory*. If all else fails, consult the *Directory of Directories* for guidance.

What Have They Done Lately?

If this is a large national company, it may have been mentioned in magazine articles during the past few years. Look up the industry or any topic related to the company's products or services in the *Readers' Guide to Periodical Literature* or *Business Periodical Index*.

If your interview is with Eli Lilly or Merck Sharp & Dohme, for instance, look up "Pharmaceuticals" or "Drugs." If it's with a company that you know manufactures contraceptives, look up "Birth Control." Or if the employer manufactures antidepressants, look up that topic as well as "Depression." What you're looking for are news or feature articles that mention the company, its products or services. You may also find quotes from corporate executives that will give you a feel for its place in the industry and perhaps its stand on certain issues.

Newspaper articles are good sources of information too. Companies that make national news can be researched by consulting the *New York Times Index*. If you're more likely to find out about this employer in your hometown daily, ask your librarian if the local paper is on microfilm. There may not be an index, so try to establish when the company might have been in the news before beginning your search.

How Are They Doing?

The corporation's annual report will give you financial information, but you may not want to request it directly. Instead have a friend who's a student (or will pose as a student) call the company's public relations department. She can explain that she's working on a term paper or other research project about the banking, cable TV or telecommunications industry—whatever business this company happens to be in—and ask them to send her a copy of the annual report and any other printed information available on current products or services. They won't be suspicious that she needs the material right away; students often wait until the last minute, and you may get press releases or brochures that offer a wealth of useful data. Ask for recent issues of the employee newspaper too.

If the company doesn't release sales figures or publish an annual report, or if it's too small to be listed in the usual directories, you can still do some financial snooping. Ask an account officer at your bank to do you a favor and get a Dun & Bradstreet report on the company. It costs them under $5 and will tell you the company's history, products, services, major developments, and financial situation.

What Is it Like Working There?

If you know someone who works for this company, talk to him or her. Otherwise, ask friends and business associates if they know anyone who does or who has worked there in the recent past. Just be sure the person you talk to isn't part of the same department in which you'll be interviewing. If so,

you'd have to be absolutely sure he or she could be trusted
not to reveal your conversation.

Ask what he likes and doesn't like about working there.
Does the company have any unusual expectations, like extremely long office hours? Does it have an industry reputation
you should know about—perhaps as a brainpicker? What are
the top executives like? How is the department you'd be
working in regarded by other departments?

On the positive side, what areas of the company are growing fastest? What products or services are considered most
important? What new areas is the company considering
going into in the future? How do people dress for work—
formally or informally, conservatively or fashionably? Do
people work with their office doors open or closed? Does
this company promote from within? Have many people been
with the company for ten years or longer? That's a sign of
stability.

Talk to the Competition

If you're interviewing at Hertz, talk to someone who works
for Avis. If you're up for a marketing spot at Federal Express,
find a friend who's with Emery. They're very likely to know
how the competition is doing and what working there would
be like. They may have interviewed there themselves.

If the company is a major advertiser, you can learn about
their current areas of emphasis by looking at magazine, newspaper and TV ads. Is Samsonite pushing its soft-sided casual
luggage by spending millions on TV commercials this year,
or concentrating on its traditional vinyl lines? Is BMW fo-
cusing on the business market with ads in *Forbes* and *Frequent Flyer,* or hoping to attract female customers by putting
some of its ad budget into *Vogue*? Even if you're interviewing
with a small local company, its newspaper ads can reveal
something about the markets it wants to reach and the image
it wants to convey.

Who's Interviewing You?

"It all boils down to chemistry," one executive search consultant points out. Either the hiring manager likes you or he/she doesn't. But wouldn't it be nice to know something about the person on the other side of that desk?

If the interviewer is a vice president or other corporate officer, he or she is likely to be listed in *Standard & Poors Register of Directors and Executives*. You can find out what schools the executive attended and what professional associations he belongs to.

Even more information is available in the library's various *Who's Who* guides. If you know the recruiter's or hiring manager's name, you may be able to learn where that person went to college and worked in the past. If you both started out as department store buyers or if you once attended a summer session at the interviewer's alma mater, you may want to bring it up.

How you put employer research to use is up to you. It may help you decide whether this is an organization you want to join. It may help you develop intelligent interview questions. Or it may simply give you more insight into the people and situations you're likely to encounter at this company.

One word of caution: Don't use your research to "show off" or make a speech about your newly-found knowledge. Bring it up only when you can tie in this information with your experience and qualifications, or as a point of reference for a question about the job. No matter how much you've learned by reading and asking about this corporation, the people who work there know much more.

STEP 20

Handle the Interview

Why: This is it.

Time: As long as it takes—and as many interviews as it takes. Some interviewees report having seen as many as 11 people in one company.

Preparation for the interview should start the night before. Lay out your interview outfit and check to be sure every garment is clean, pressed, and perfect. Have your shoes shined, or do them yourself. Women may want to tuck an extra pair of pantyhose into purse or portfolio in case of a last-minute run or snag.

If you wake up on interview morning to find an eight-inch snowfall or a strike on the commuter train you always take, get there anyway. Leave early and walk, rent a car or call a friend, but do whatever it takes to make it to the appointed place.

Arrive on time. In fact, if you're there five minutes early, you'll have a chance to put away your coat, umbrella and any other bulky gear in the reception area closet. Just to be safe, take a minute in the washroom to comb your hair, straighten your tie and put yourself into a job-getting frame of mind.

When you're called in, enter the manager's office confidently, shake hands firmly and take a seat. Put your plans into action and get your three main points across in response to the interviewer's questions. You can relax because you're prepared for this, but keep the 20 commandments of job interviewing in mind.

1. *Don't use profanity,* even if the interviewer swears like a sailor.
2. *Don't smoke,* unless the job is with a tobacco company.
3. *Don't make jokes,* but always laugh at the interviewer's.
4. *Don't bring up politics, religion or sex.*
5. *Don't take ten minutes to answer the first question.* One-sentence answers sound abrupt, but going on for paragraphs is long-winded.
6. *Don't try to run things.* Interrupting with something like "Before we get to my experience, I have a few questions about this job" just turns off recruiters. Controlling an interview the right way means following the employer's agenda, but working in your points.
7. *Do ask questions*—in an appropriate manner. When the interviewer asks if you have questions, it's time to say something like, "Could you tell me about the department's working relationship with Marketing?" or "Is this a newly-created job, or has the person who handled it before gone on to something new?"
8. *Don't get personal with the interviewer.* Asking whether she's married, how long she's been with the company and whether she lives in the suburbs might be friendly interest. But it could just as easily come off as nosy and impertinent.
9. *Don't recite the annual report.* "I noticed recently that your gross sales last year were $3.6 billion" is an obvious effort to impress the interviewer and can have the opposite effect. Read the annual report to familiarize yourself with the company, then develop an intelligent question, not a show-off comment.
10. *Don't dismiss or discredit any interviewer.* Never be rude or discourteous to anyone involved in the selection process, even if you think the person is not

very bright. That "ignorant clerk" may have the ear of your prospective supervisor.

11. *Don't relax until you've got the offer.* Jobs have been lost at the very last minute. Candidates have gone on what were planned to be courtesy interviews, with the boss's boss or associate, then made bad impressions and have blown the whole deal. Headhunters suggest you stay on your toes until you have a company ID in your wallet.

12. *Don't criticize your present employer.*

13. *Don't insult the interviewer's company.* "I know your division has serious sales problems, but I know just what you need" is an approach born to fail.

14. *Don't name-drop.* The big executive you know in this company, or in another part of the industry, may be the interviewer's worst enemy.

15. *Don't lose your cool.* Never get angry during an interview, even if you think the interviewer has become possessed by the devil and is questioning your mother's moral character. Some companies "stress interview" to see if a candidate will be able to maintain his or her composure in tough situations.

16. *Don't ask about benefits.* Questions about vacation policies, medical packages and retirement plans give the impression that you're more interested in security than in doing a great job. You'll have plenty of time to ask about benefits once an offer has been made.

17. *Do empathize.* Try to put yourself in the interviewer's place and ask yourself what this supervisor needs and is looking for. It can help you come up with the right answers.

18. *Do use body language to get the job.* Sit up straight and slightly forward to show interest. Really listen to the interviewer, and let your face show that you're attentive.

19. *Never relax and have a good time.* Don't let your hair down and talk about your true feelings, even if the interviewer seems to encourage it. "Yes, my husband and I do enjoy sailing" is a perfectly appropriate answer to a question about private life, but try to turn the subject back to business. "We miss it now, but

we both wanted to live closer to the downtown area. We both spend such long hours at our offices."

20. *Do put on an act.* This is not to say you should be dishonest, but the purpose of the interview is to put your best foot forward. Convince this person that you want this job and will be perfect for it, even if you haven't completely decided that you do or will be.

'I SEE YOU HAVE TWO SMALL CHILDREN'

Sex, race and age discrimination are all illegal in the workplace, but they still go on. Most personnel department and employment agency people have had the legalities drummed into their heads for years. They know better than to risk their jobs by asking who's going to take care of the kids when you go back to work. But the nonpersonnel people who make the final decision on hiring you aren't always so savvy.

What should you do if you run into an interviewer who asks your age, your husband's occupation or your method of birth control? Most career counselors suggest you answer politely: "Oh, there are no problems there that would affect my handling this job."

Then if you don't get the job, you can consider filing a formal complaint. If you do get hired, play it by ear, depending upon your reporting relationship to the offending party. Or take the advice of executive search consultant William Morin of Drake, Beam, Morin: "Work your way up to the top of the company and fire the idiot who did it."

DON'T CALL US, WE'LL CALL YOU

Before you leave the interview, get a feel for what your follow-up procedure should be. Just ask, "Could you tell me what your timing is?" or "What would be a good time for me to call you about this?" The interviewer will almost always let you know in no uncertain terms what the situation is and whether she'll welcome follow-up calls. You may be asked to phone the personnel department instead. If you're working through an agency or search firm, they'll handle contact for you.

Should you send a thank-you note? "Not if that's all it is," says one personnel officer. "A pure thank-you note is an anachronism, like wearing little white gloves to the interview." Instead send a letter to the hiring manager reiterating a point made during the interview:

Dear Mr. Parker:
Thank you again for taking the time on Tuesday to discuss the Sales Manager's position with me.
I'm glad we had a chance to talk about the company's North American expansion at some length. As I mentioned, I believe my experience on the West Coast, especially in the San Francisco market, would enable me to make a valuable contribution to that effort.
I hope you agree. I'll look forward to hearing from your office or from Ms. Jenkins of Gaines-Oppenheim.

> Sincerely,

cc: Bonnie S. Jenkins

If you're being considered for the spot, chances are good that you'll be called in for several interviews. Written thank-you's obviously aren't necessary after each meeting.

DEALING WITH REJECTION

What's the worst thing that can happen? The search firm can call and tell you that you didn't get the job. You can call the hiring manager only to learn that they've chosen someone else. Or you can get the bad news by mail. No matter how it happens, it never feels good.

To keep up your morale (an absolute necessity for continued job hunting), remind yourself of a few truths:

- It happens to everybody. Nobody gets 14 interviews and 14 job offers.
- It probably had nothing to do with your ability to do good work. People lose out on jobs because the manager secretly wanted to hire a woman, a man, a Black, someone older, someone younger, a Libra or someone named Heather.
- Going through the interviewing process has just made you that much more adept at it. You'll be even better the next time.

Don't be caught on rejection day with no other irons in the fire. No matter how sure you are that this job is in the bag, continue to make contacts, answer ads, send résumés and work with agencies or search firms. Even if the offer does come through, you can use all these contacts when it's time for the next move up the ladder.

21

Name Your Salary

Why: This is what you're working for. When you're talking money, the job offer is in sight.

Time: Two seconds

The headhunter hung up the phone and frowned. "That was a woman who answered an ad last week for a $40,000 job we had," he explained to the job hunter seated on the other side of the desk. "The spot was just filled and I told her. So she asked me about an ad we ran this week for a $25,000 job. Who is she trying to kid?"

In today's business world the people who hire expect you to know what you're worth—and to stick to it. Fortunately, there are formulas for demanding an appropriate salary.

If you're earning $20,000 now, but a classified ad describing a perfect job that pays $30,000 catches your eye, should you bother to answer it? Probably, if your qualifications measure up to what the ad demands—but you're bucking the formula. You're asking for a 50 percent increase!

In recent years the average increase when switching jobs has been 10–15 percent. That is, if you're currently earning $20,000, a new employer would expect to have to offer you $22,000–$23,000 to make the change worth your while. Inflation, however, has taken its toll and some personnel executives report that 15–25 percent increases have become much more common. So the person earning $20,000 may now be able to command $23,000–$25,000 when changing jobs. A

$30,000 employee can ask as much as $37,500, and a $50,000 person, $62,500. Bigger increases are exceptional cases.

SHOULD YOU GO FOR THE BIG MONEY?

When answering a classified ad, there's no harm in shooting for the moon. In working with an agency or search firm—or making personal job contacts—you should demand a much higher salary only if you're willing to settle for nothing less. Take this gamble only if you're a perfect or near-perfect match for the kind of job you're looking for.

HOW MUCH ARE YOU WORTH AS A NEW GRADUATE?

If you're just out of high school or college with no full-time business experience, there are several ways to estimate your market value. Scan classified ads in your local newspaper for any beginners' salaries listed in your occupation. Check the *Occupational Outlook Handbook* or *90 Most Promising Careers for the 80s* (Monarch Press) for starting salaries. National averages for many careers are listed. Or get in touch with a professional association in your career field for their estimate.

SHOULD YOU GIVE OUT SALARY HISTORY?

Career counselors are evenly divided on the question. If an ad asks for salary history and 200 of the 400 respondents don't comply, it's easy for the recruiter or hiring manager to eliminate that half from consideration. Others suggest that you avoid coming in too high or too low simply by stating, "My salary is competitive" in your cover letter. In interviews, the same people recommend answering the question with a question of your own, "What is the range for this job?"

It's true that most large companies have a formalized system of salary ranges, based on a written analysis of duties and responsibilities. If the job is a "level 10" with a range of $27,800–$35,100, it would take something akin to an act of Congress to get you $40,000. It's unusual for people to be hired at the top of the range, much less above it; there's no room for merit increases.

Demanding to know the range, instead of responding to the original question, can appear hostile to some interviewers, however. You'll probably know something about the range before the interview. If you don't, a better answer might be "I'm currently earning $26,000, but my asking salary would depend on a number of factors, including the opportunities this job might offer for growth and advancement."

If your most recent salary was 10–25 percent lower than the quoted salary for this job, you have nothing to hide. Give a straight answer.

SHOULD YOU EVER LIE ABOUT SALARY?

Not a good idea. Many employers won't reveal past salary figures, but résumé private eyes could find you out. Do add in your Christmas bonus or other special payments when quoting salary, however.

SHOULD YOU EVER TAKE A PAY CUT?

Yes, if you're making a career switch of any kind. A large percentage of successful people have done it at one time or another. The only way to make a switch without losing money may be to transfer from one department to the other within the same company. Personnel might agree to a lateral move, because they know your work.

WHEN SHOULD YOU TALK SALARY?

Not until you're sure the hiring manager wants you. And in most cases let her bring up the subject. If you're working with an agency or search firm, they may handle all salary negotiations.

Most people work because they have to, but salary isn't everything. Be ready to consider the value of benefits like profit-sharing and medical coverage, and of perks like expense accounts and corporate discounts. A new career opportunity should be part of your financial consideration, even if it doesn't mean more money right now. It does mean more impressive credentials, and that will translate into dollars and cents on all the paychecks ahead.